....

....

....

....

AUTHOR .... bris

TITLE .... French plan

CL. 791 436

ESSION NO. 05

FRENCH
FILM NOIR

Robin Buss

FRENCH FILM NOIR

Marion Boyars

London · New York

First published in Great Britain and
in the United States in 1994
by Marion Boyars Publishers

24 Lacy Road London SW15 1NL
237 East 39th Street, New York, NY 10016

British Library Cataloguing in Publication Data
Robin Buss
French Film Noir
I.   Title
791.430944

Library of Congress Cataloging-in-Publication Data
French film noir/Robin Buss
Includes bibliographical references and index.
1. Film noir--France--History and criticism.   I. Title.
PN1995.9.F54B87   1994
791.43'655--dc20   93-28651

ISBN 0-7145-2963-X Hardcover

Typeset in Baskerville and Rockwell
by Ann Buchan (Typesetters), Shepperton
Printed and bound by
Biddles Ltd, Guildford and King's Lynn

CONTENTS

ACKNOWLEDGEMENTS

The author and publishers would like to thank Artificial Eye Film Company, MK2 and Nouvelles Editions de Films for permission to use photographs.

Every effort has been made to trace the present copyright holders of stills. The author and publishers apologise for any unintentional omission or neglect and will be pleased to insert the appropriate acknowledgement in any subsequent edition of the book.

I.

IN BLACK AND WHITE

'Nothing,' Shelley wrote, 'can exceed the grandeur and energy of the character of the Devil as expressed in *Paradise Lost*.' This was in 1819 or 1820 in Shelley's essay ('On the Devil and Devils'), the purpose of which was ironic: to ridicule Christian belief. The remark about the character of the Devil, however, is a commonplace, already noted by most earlier writers on Milton, who debated whether Satan or Adam could be described as the 'hero' of his Christian epic. The 'grandeur' and 'energy' of evil are a central proposition of *film noir*.

Before we start to examine it, some attempts at definitions. The term '*film noir*' was coined by French critics during the 1940s, to describe a particular type of crime fiction. Though the phrase itself is French, it was at the start associated with an American genre that arose out of American experience during the 1920s and 1930s, on which it drew either directly or indirectly, in adaptations from writers like James M. Cain, Dashiell Hammett and Raymond Chandler. Its setting was urban, its subject matter was violence and its underlying ethos was cynicism about human motives, morals and social behaviour. The protagonists could be gangsters or loners (though, in a sense, they were always alone); they might be clearly on the wrong side of the law; or on the right side; or, in the case of the private eye, the archetypal *film noir* hero, hover ambiguously between law-breakers and law-enforcers. If they upheld the law, they might eventually be rewarded by unmasking the criminals and vindicating themselves (though the motives of the private eye are often suspect); if they transgressed, they might receive their just deserts, though not always by due process of law. The central character in James M. Cain's *The Postman Always Rings Twice* is punished, but for the crime he did not commit. This novel was one of the first in the genre to attract European film-makers: Pierre Chenal adapted it to a French setting in *Le Dernier tournant* (1939), Luchino Visconti set it on the banks of the Po for *Ossessione* (1942), before any American studio decided to tackle Cain's fatalistic story of sexual obsession.

The originality and the salient characteristics of this type of American fiction were perceived more clearly from a distance, in Europe, than they were in America itself. The gangster films of the 1930s depicted criminals, particularly those active during the years of Prohibition, as belonging to a violent sub-culture which needed to be brought under control, while endowing them with glamour: they had money, women, fast cars, tommy-guns and a power derived from their contempt for conventional morality. In order to combat them, the agents of law and order needed to adopt similar methods and to blend into the urban jungle. Even when the police are not corrupt, their behaviour is ambivalent. *Film noir* extends this ambivalence to the heart of its moral universe.

The gangster films grew out of a specifically American experience, but the underlying mood of cynicism and despair that Europeans detected in them exercized a powerful appeal. Europe in the 1930s may not have been confronted with a crime wave on the American scale, but it was addressing questions of social and political morality, the morality of power and the place of the individual in relation to an increasingly oppressive and impersonal state. *Le Dernier tournant* shows a couple driven to murder by desire; the corollary of their desire is a frustration which is sexual, but also more than sexual. She is trapped in a marriage with an older and, by implication, impotent or homosexual man, while her lover is unemployed: in both cases, economic forces have denied them the opportunity to build 'normal' lives, and passion is a means of escape, if not a solution. In the end, like the characters that Jean Gabin was playing in the 'poetic realist' films of the same period, fate serves as the mechanism which confronts them with the reality of their situation.

There is also, already, a sense in which they are not only victims of fate, but victims of roles they have chosen. By the late 1930s, the most popular means of escape from the frustrations of daily life was the cinema, which offered the audience images of glamour and sexual passion. Dress, speech, attitudes, aspirations and manners were influenced by what occurred on the screen, which made it a source of concern to moralists. Few people (ordinary members of the public, film directors and scriptwriters, or even aspiring gangsters) have the opportunity to observe how 'real' criminals behave (or are 'meant to' behave), so we have to rely on fictional images. Even before the 1960s and the films of Godard, when the imitation became explicit, these characters appear to be at least subliminally copying each other, or earlier, often foreign, models.

There are moral implications to this playing of roles: the 'hero' of *Le Dernier tournant* feels no remorse for his crime, but goes towards the guillotine still obsessed with the woman for whom he committed it, still a victim of his *amour fou*. But audiences could see beyond the individual fate of the characters. 'That's France!', an Italian woman exclaimed at the

Venice Biennale, after seeing Marcel Carné's *Quai des Brumes* (1938) — just as French spectators at Warner Bros films like *Angels with Dirty Faces* (1938) would have thought: 'that's America!' The urban environment of the American city represented the essence of modern life, characterized by the breakdown of traditional moral and family values, impersonality and mechanization, just as in the previous century Paris, through the novels of Eugène Sue or the poetry of Baudelaire, had become the site of a comparable feeling of individual alienation and loneliness. The introduction of artificial lighting in cities meant that life there could continue, ignoring the natural cycles of activity and repose that ruled in the country and giving opportunities for vice, murder and theft. Night in the city, the city after dark, *dans le noir*, is a focus of special anxiety, melancholy and spleen — as Baudelaire said, 'bringing rest to some and, to others, care'.

A century earlier, too, Edgar Allen Poe had chosen Paris as the setting for what is often considered the first modern detective story, 'The Murders in the Rue Morgue'. The classic detective story is an intellectual puzzle with the detective as hero, but the extent of his heroism depends on the ingenuity of the villain who has set the puzzle, and whose grandeur and energy, as prime mover, constantly challenges the hero's prestige. From Balzac's Vautrin onwards, the master criminal always threatens to become a more interesting figure than the great detective. By the turn of the century, Maurice Leblanc's 'gentleman crook', Arsène Lupin, Marcel Allain's Fantômas, and Gaston Leroux's pair of amateur detective, Rouletabille, and 'amateur' criminal, Chéri-Bibi ('amateur', because more a victim of circumstances than intrinsically evil), blur the lines between the forces of the law and those opposed to them; all were to become enduring figures in the media of cinema and television.

This is to say that ambivalence (or even what might more pretentiously be called the existential concerns) of *film noir* are perceptible in some detective fiction, notably where it crosses over into the thriller, a genre developed from nineteenth-century melodrama and pulp fiction. The merging of the two genres was inevitable, given their shared concern with crime and punishment; and, fuelling both, is the desire of readers for thrills. A lurid murder story may ostensibly set out to prove that crime doesn't pay, but I can see nothing to support the idea that readers have ever bought such books in order to be persuaded of that or to reassure themselves about the efficiency of the police. Much of the criticism that used to be levelled against pulp fiction, and the criticism that is still levelled against screen violence, ignores the resolution of the plot and assumes that what people enjoy is the excitement of criminal violence; and rightly so. Again, it is clear that the expected equation doesn't work: the greater the power of the criminal, the more he or she exhibits the grandeur and energy of evil, the more this should enhance the prestige of the detective who overcomes him; but, in reality, it serves to underline the daring of those who transgress.

There is another reason, which is that (especially perhaps at certain times), we are easily persuaded of the supremacy of evil and the amorality of the universe. This is one argument used to support the view that films like those of Chenal or Carné were appropriate to the mood of the moment in France during the late 1930s. The argument is sometimes couched in terms of 'realism': like the naturalistic novels of Zola towards the end of the nineteenth century, films or novels that showed people struggling against a grim environment and succumbing to impersonal forces, were felt to be closer to everyday reality than those that showed them controlling their lives, overcoming problems and frustrations, and achieving happy endings. France during the 1930s knew economic depression and corrupt government; the hope, then the deception of the Popular Front; the rise of fascism in Italy, Germany and Spain; the gathering threat of war. Ordinary French working people might not have been in precisely the situation of the worker driven to murder in *Le*

Jour se lève or the deserter in *Quai des Brumes*, but they could believe in the fatality that put Jean Gabin in these predicaments more easily than they could in the characters of Jean Dréville's 1937 Imperial Russian drama, *Les Nuits blanches de Saint-Pétersbourg*.

Obviously, questions of 'realism' and 'escapism' in fiction are problematic — and become more so the closer you cut it, for example in drama-documentary, or documentary itself. Audiences did not necessarily prefer realism. They often preferred escape and one can argue that, the more threatening the reality of the time, the more they will tend to do so. But there was a growing public in France for the relative amorality and 'realistic' violence of American films; and, once the milieu and the ethos had been established, there was a readership, too, for American hard-boiled fiction. The *roman noir* and the *film noir* feed off each other, the first providing the second with material, while adapting its narrative style to make it more 'cinematic'. Readers are also cinemagoers and can visualize the scenes of a novel as though they were watching them on the screen, while at the same time the novel's greater freedom from censorship means that it is usually in advance of film, preparing the readers and helping them to decode what they see.

The audience for American crime fiction, once established in the cinema, was abruptly frustrated. From 1940, the German Occupation put an end to the importing of American films. Immediately, the French film industry tried to fill the gap, with fantasies and detective stories. More interesting, however, in the present context, was the creation of the 'Collection Minuit', a series of thrillers written by French writers under American-sounding pseudonyms. This might be seen as both the rival and the successor to an earlier series, 'Le Masque', founded in 1927 and specializing in country-house detective stories, usually with an English setting (the cinematic equivalent being Marcel Carné's film *Drôle de drame*, 1937). But the 'Collection Minuit' faced resolutely across the Atlantic and, with 'midnight' in its title, became the immediate predecessor of the most famous collection of all in the field, the 'Série Noire' created by Marcel Duhamel in 1945. The *roman noir* existed, *film noir* was soon to follow.

The *film noir*, when the term entered the language a couple of years later, was thus the cinematic equivalent of the *roman (de la Série) Noir(e)*: not a detective puzzle, but crime fiction, with an urban setting and cynical outlook on life, specifically American in ethos (even though two authors of *romans noirs* much admired and translated in France, James Hadley Chase and Peter Cheyney, were English). If French writers wrote for the series (and only one was permitted to do so before 1950), they wrote under English/American names. To be authentic, *roman noir* — and consequently *film noir* — had to be American; so how, for the purposes of this book, can we justify applying the term to French films?

One answer is simply that, in the past 45 years, the meaning of the term has changed, and the influence of the genre has been such that one can see its central concerns extended to a wide range of different types of film. *Film noir*, Michael Walker declares in *The Movie Book of Film Noir*, is not a genre, but a 'generic field'. It is more important for the time being to state where its centre lies. In a sense, this entire book will be an extended definition of the genre, rather than starting with one; because, like any genre, *film noir* (or the crime thriller, gangster film, detective story, police procedural, murder story, political thriller, *policier*, *polar* — all of which can contain elements derived from American *film noir* of the 1940s), develops by experiment and reaction, in relation to what has gone before. The fact that the genre was first named in France and its creators given serious critical attention there, suggests that it had a special relevance to the French context. What French film-makers did with the genre, having sensed that their American counterparts had something special to say through it about crime and punishment, is the subject of this book.

'*Questo non è l'Italia!*', Mussolini's son, Vittorio, exclaimed as he walked out of the 1942 première of *Ossessione*, neatly paralleling the reaction of his compatriot who had declared four years earlier that *Quai des Brumes* 'was France'. Most Europeans were agreed that Hollywood gave an authentic representation of American reality; but they were less willing to see themselves in bleakly amoral stories of domestic violence and sexual repression. Not that Europe itself was especially placid during these years, but the patriotic savagery of war made the authorities even more sensitive than usual to negative depictions of the societies they were defending.

Henri-Georges Clouzot began his career in cinema as a scriptwriter, notably adapting Simenon's novel *Les Inconnus dans la maison* (Henri Decoin, 1941), which was made by Continental during the Occupation. The Nazi Propaganda Staffel had at first tried to replace the banned American films with German ones, but found that they were unpopular; so, in 1941, they authorized the resumption of film-making in French studios, naturally keeping a close watch on what was produced. As any realistic depiction of current events was dangerous, the industry turned to relatively safe genres like the detective story.

Simenon's work was already an established part of the canon. Inspector Maigret made his first screen appearances in Jean Tarride's *Le Chien jaune* and Jean Renoir's *La Nuit du carrefour*, both in 1932. The actor Pierre Renoir, in the second of these, became the most celebrated Maigret of the decade. He was followed by Harry Baur, Michel Simon, Albert Préjean, Jean Gabin and others. Maigret would later achieve success on both television and outside France: Burgess Meredith played him in his own film, *The Man on the Eiffel Tower* (1949), Rupert Davies in the popular British television series of the 1960s, Michael Gambon in the considerably less popular series in 1992. There were also television adaptations in the USA, the USSR, Japan, Holland, Germany and Italy. On French television, the part was given to Jean

Richard in a series of nearly 90 episodes betwen 1967 and 1990, then to Bruno Cremer from 1992 onwards.

For foreigners, the French (provincial or Parisian) settings are part of the appeal, reflecting the personality of the man, a middle-aged, pipe-smoking detective who enjoys all the things that make life bearable for the French middle classes — most of all, *la cuisine bourgeoise* provided by Mme Maigret. He has numerous counterparts, for example in films by Claude Chabrol. The policeman played by Alec McCowan in Alfred Hitchcock's *Frenzy* (1972) is a conscious tribute, with the ironic footnote that the Englishman loves plain English cooking, while his wife is taking a course in French *haute cuisine* and insists on serving him dishes of shellfish or small birds, in which their mortal remains are visible, imperfectly disguised.

Maigret has gone through so many transformations, and become so much a stock figure, that one is likely to forget the originality of the character. The detective created by Simenon differed from his predecessors: he was not a private eye, but a policeman, with an office at the Quai des Orfèvres, who solved crimes by penetrating the psychology of the criminal. Where Sherlock Holmes had used forensic science to distance himself from evil and analyze the criminal's method, Maigret pursues the motive and is consequently led to ask questions about human nature. *Tout comprendre, c'est tout pardonner*: behind the stolid bourgeois façade is an understanding of the extremes of behaviour which precludes condemnation. If Maigret pursues wrongdoing, it is more with the sorrow of a priest than the anger of a judge.

Immediately before *Les Inconnus dans la maison*, Clouzot wrote a screenplay from a novel by Stanislas-André Steeman, *Le Dernier des six* (Georges Lacombe, 1941), with Pierre Fresnay in the leading role. Then, for his first film as director, he suggested to Steeman a further adaptation with Fresnay. Steeman's mystery, *L'Assassin habite au 21*, was a deliberate homage to the English detective story, set in a seedy London boarding house and shrouded in the inevitable

London fog. The circumstances of the time made it impossible to use this original setting, so Clouzot transfers the story to Paris and fills the boarding house with Parisian characters: a violinist who makes dolls, a blind man, an alcoholic veteran of the previous war. The resulting comedy-thriller has elements of the American 1930s series, *The Thin Man*, but filmed in an expressionist style that foreshadows Clouzot's subsequent films.

Maigret, or the detectives played by Fresnay in this film and by Louis Jouvet in Clouzot's later adaptation of a novel by Steeman, *Quai des Orfèvres* (1947), are superficially reassuring: by unravelling the mystery, they demonstrate the power of the police force to which they belong and the triumph of law over crime. But in order to do so, they have to acknowledge the fact that the authority of the law is not absolute (crimes are committed), and to enter the world of the criminal. They are tainted by this association with evil, they share the thoughts and feelings of the murderer, they discover him behind his deceptively commonplace disguise. Again, the detective's ingenuity is conditional on the ingenuity of the criminal: the prime mover in the classic detective story is Satan, who creates the universe in which the characters move.

'You think that goodness is light and darkness evil,' says a character in Clouzot's second film, *Le Corbeau* (1943). 'But where is the light? Where is the darkness?' Situated between these two fairly conventional detective stories and based on a poison pen case of the 1930s in Tulle, *Le Corbeau* has some structural affinities with the typical investigation film: a cast of likely suspects is progressively eliminated, until (for reasons of suspense) the culprit is finally revealed as the least probable suspect of all. 'For reasons of suspense': the mechanics of plot in these tales habitually require the blurring of distinctions between 'light' and 'dark' characters. The investigator's cliché is: 'I suspect everyone' — and rightly so, given the conventions of the genre; but the idea that 'everyone is suspect' has far-reaching implications, because the assumptions that we bring to the cinema (which make a suspect likely or not), reflect the existing social order. The least likely suspect is the most conventionally 'respectable', so one can see that a mere device for increasing suspense may be potentially subversive.

The producers, Continental, compounded their misdemeanour by advertising the setting of *Le Corbeau* as 'a small town *like so many in France*'. The film was condemned by the forces of the Right (the morality expressed in the Vichy slogan *Travail, Famille, Patrie* was deeply offended by this picture of *La France profonde*), and given the highest (i.e., most condemnatory) ratings by the two bodies which vetted films: the Catholic Office rated it 5 ('forbidden'), the Office Familial de Documentation Artistique went one better and gave it 6 (when 5 meant 'not suitable [even] for adult audiences'). The right-wing press said that the film 'infringed the most elementary principles of the most ordinary morality'. This did not mean, however, that it won the approval of the Resistance and the left. The clandestine *Lettres françaises* saw the 'morally crippled, abnormal and corrupt characters' in the film as a subtle piece of anti-French, therefore pro-Nazi propaganda, and Clouzot continued to be attacked after the Liberation for alleged 'intellectual collaboration', because the film was supposed to have been distributed in Germany to reinforce negative images of France. What distressed both sides was the author-director's bleak view of human nature. Collaborators and Resistants differed in the way they understood the soul of the nation, but neither wished to be told, even through a work of fiction, that the prize for which they were struggling was corrupt.

Of course, *Le Corbeau* could not be exported outside the Axis countries and after the Liberation it was temporarily banned. Clouzot went on to make an adaptation of Abbé Prévost's novel *Manon Lescaut* (1949), updated to postwar France, and a farce, *Miquette et sa mère* (1949). It was only through his two major films of the 1950s that he began to have an impact abroad, but the effect was for a time to make his work stand as the epitome of postwar French cinema. The ethics of the films and the genre remained a matter of concern to critics and audiences.

This concern is difficult to appreciate today, but it is worth trying to do so. The first of the films, *Le Salaire de la peur* (1953), is a suspense thriller set in an unnamed South American country, where four unemployed exiles agree to drive two trucks of nitroglycerine to an oil well in the interior where it is needed to blow out a fire. Like gangsters planning one final job, the four (two Frenchmen, an Italian and a German, played by Yves Montand, Charles Vanel, Folco Lulli and Peter van Eyck) hope that the money they earn on this dangerous mission will allow them to realize their dreams of escape to some better life; as in most gangster films based on this proposition, they are destined to fail — the difference being that the moral in the gangster film is that 'the wages of *sin* are death' or that 'crime doesn't pay', while the moral here is that 'there is no escape'.

Because it portrays a US oil company in a banana republic, the reaction from some quarters was to condemn the film as anti-American and anti-capitalist. Even this does not quite explain the virulence of *Time* magazine (February 21, 1955): 'a picture that is one of the most evil ever made', 'sophisticated in evil', 'lies and filth', with propaganda that 'is mostly vicious and irresponsible, occasionally clear-sighted, always original', by a director who manipulates his camera 'with malevolent dexterity'. The satanic nature of the work is actually confirmed by the director's skill: 'one of the great shockers of all time . . . the suspense it creates is close to prostrating.' Clouzot, the writer concludes, 'does not seem to care what happens to human consciousness and the culture it has laboured to create' (French critics, referring particularly to the death of the character played by Charles Vanel, called it 'atheistic').

In Britain, *Le Salaire de la peur* was chosen to re-open the Academy Cinema in Oxford Street, London, which had been closed for redecoration and was to become an important venue for continental European films. British critics were less concerned by the ideological message, but some were no less extreme in their reactions. *The Daily Mirror* (May 26, 1954), in an article headlined 'Children Must Not See This' (the film had been given an A certificate, which meant that under-18s could watch it if accompanied by an adult), spoke of 'unnecessary nudity' and 'violence that will make you shudder'. Campbell Dixon, in *The Daily Telegraph*, called it 'sadistic', 'sordid' and 'cruel', but 'by the standards of the screen, a masterpiece' — again awarding high marks for technical achievement, and none for morality. The ending, in which the last of the four drivers is killed, 'has been condemned as the film's last wanton cruelty', but Dixon was 'now more inclined to see it as one moral gesture'.

The motive for the outrage is Clouzot's depiction of his four characters as men driven by a primitive desire to survive. At one point in the film, the older Frenchman (Vanel) is trapped under the wheels of the truck in a mounting pool of oil, flowing out of a pipeline that has been fractured by the explosion of the preceding lorry. His younger companion (Montand) has to decide whether to stop the truck and let it become irretrievably bogged down, or drive on over the older man's leg. He drives on: in some circumstances, the younger generation must sacrifice the old. Once the truck is free, he goes back, retrieves his companion and nurses him in his arms until he dies.

A modern spectator would have to watch very hard indeed to see any 'unnecessary nudity', but the sexual undertones of the film are unmistakeable. As the journey begins, Montand casts aside the woman he has been living with, who is pleading for him not to take part in the mission. Later, the homoerotic bond between the four men is made more explicit by a ritual in which three of them urinate together, but punish Vanel, who has proved to be the weak member of the team, by telling him to *aller pisser en Suisse* - in other words, sending him to Coventry. The one moment of tenderness comes with Vanel's death. Otherwise, Clouzot sees human relationships in terms of a struggle for survival.

The film was judged to contain 'material offending to an American audience', and cut. When it was finally shown in New York at its full running time of 148 minutes, *The Village Voice* (October 22, 1991) saw it as a reflection of Fifties 'nuclear anxiety' and, in passing, condemned it as 'aggressively pan-European and openly racist' (because of its attitude to the native Indian population of the country where it is set). One ideological sin replaces another.

Just because times and attitudes have changed, it would be wrong to dismiss all contemporary criticism of *Le Salaire de la peur* as misjudged: the film is bleak, resolutely materialistic and, at times, contains elements of sadism. Though not a murder story, it has many characteristics that we shall find in other *films noirs*: suspense, sexual undercurrents, cynicism about human motivation, a sense of fatality, a grim view of human existence. The film's early critics were not wrong to see Clouzot's universe as godless and amoral.

They did take it seriously, as an (existentialist) philosophical statement about the human condition, as well as a suspense movie, though some were inclined to see the long preliminary section, establishing the men's situation in the desolate township, as unnecessarily retarding the action. Clouzot's film benefitted with British and American critics from the extraordinary intellectual prestige enjoyed by Paris in the postwar years, and from being made in the rather vague genre of 'suspense thriller' rather than the more specific one of 'detective/murder story'. Even a well-made, well-acted, well-scripted American *film noir* could be dismissed by a 'serious' British critic as 'a modest film, a mere thriller' (C. A. Lejeune, writing in *The Observer*, June 21, 1942, on *The Maltese Falcon*). Many Hollywood examples of the genre, which are now read with the same attention as critics of the 1940s and 1950s accorded to *Le Salaire de la peur*, would go more or less unnoticed, passed over as 'mere entertainment'.

The disadvantage of the genre label is clear in the reviews of Clouzot's next film, *Les Diaboliques* (1955). This was freely adapted from a novel, *Celle qui n'était plus*, by Pierre Boileau and Thomas Narcéjac, a well-known literary collaboration (and authors of the book from which Hitchcock's master-piece, *Vertigo*, was adapted). Boileau and Narcéjac's books are highly coloured psychological thrillers, with elements of Grand Guignol; this one, first published in 1952, is a murder story told in the third person, but from the point of view of the eventual victim, a middle-aged salesman married to a timid, dull wife, whom he is plotting to kill with the help of his mistress. The writers are concerned primarily with analyzing the man's unhappiness, his sexual frustration, his bleak marriage and the appeal of Lucienne, the strong-willed other woman in his life who seems to offer fulfilment and escape. From the start, his scheme goes wrong and he is caught up in a terrifying mystery: the reader shares Ravinel's bewilderment and loneliness as he struggles to keep control of events and to retain a sense of reality.

It was not possible for Clouzot, in a film, to retell the story from the viewpoint of this single consciousness (except, perhaps, through some artifical device like a voice-over narration), though he does make good use of point-of-view shots. Taking a hint from the profession of the character's father, he turns him into a teacher, rather than a salesman, and sets the action against the background of a second-rate private school: Ravinel (played by Paul Meurisse) is the bullying head, Lucienne (Simone Signoret) and the wife (Véra Clouzot), his assistants. The depressing and claustro-phobic atmosphere of the place is graphically depicted; Ravinel's frustration emerges in his spiteful treatment of his wife, and the empty premises of the school during the holiday provides an ideal setting for the melodrama of the climax. This is in many ways a model of adaptation by a film-maker (and by his co-writer, G. Geronimi) who under-stands his medium: what is inevitably lost is the novel's perspective on the character's inner thoughts and details of his past life, can be compensated for by close observation of this enviroment.

As Boileau and Narcéjac acknowledged in a preface to a re-edition of the novel (now renamed *Les Diaboliques* in deference to the film), Clouzot explores 'precisely the same idea by different means, and one could even say that, the closer the film had tried to stay faithful to the book, the more it would have had to depart from it . . . Clouzot's film is much less an adaptation than a re-creation'. As in *Le Corbeau* and *L'Assassin habite au 21*, the director also surrounds the central characters with a series of vignettes: an observant schoolboy, an eccentric teacher, a suspicious detective, a pair of old age pensioners who spend their days listening to the radio, spying on their neighbours and worrying about the plumbing. The minor characters contribute to the suspense or to the gallery of frustrated and inhibited lives.

Most French critics dismissed the film as an empty puzzle, though some Catholic writers saw it as a portrayal of evil ('our age has too often lost this sense of the diabolical'), or felt that its ingenuity in the depiction of an amoral universe made it 'all the more dangerous' to its audience. The London release was preceded by news reports from Paris, saying that the doors of cinemas were being closed from the start of the film and audiences were begged not to give away the ending. 'Mr Hitchcock will have to move over,' *The Times* proclaimed (February 9, 1955). This advance publicity certainly contributed to the success of the film when it did open: *The Daily Sketch* (December 1, 1955) called it 'the top thriller of 1955', but Alan Brien, in *The Evening Standard* on the same day found it 'a disappointment', and there was criticism of the 'synthetic thrills' (*Daily Express*), as well as irritation from reviewers who found it hard to discuss when they could not reveal the plot.

There were more interesting reactions from other quarters, particularly to the shock effects. 'Just how horrible can films get?', Reg Whiteley asked in *The Daily Mirror* (December 2, 1955), to be echoed by C. A. Lejeune in *The Observer*

(December 4, 1955): ' . . . a vogue at the moment for the horrid in entertainment'. Within a decade, Lejeune was to give up reviewing, partly because she was sickened by an increase in violence and 'immorality' in the cinema. Milton Shulman (*The Sunday Express*, December 4, 1955) remarked that 'it is no trick to sicken an audience by such blunt methods as these' and spoke of the film's 'calculated malevolence'. A year later, *Tribune* (November 16, 1956) referred to 'calculated vileness' and 'crude sensationalism', describing the film as 'vulgar and nasty, unhealthy, with a fever of calculated perversion'.

Of course, many spectators were not at all sickened by Clouzot's work: they had gone to the cinema to enjoy precisely the sensations that so upset the reviewers. And, apart from a few, like C. A. Lejeune for whom such material was truly offensive, critics were almost certainly not themselves sickened by the depiction of violence and 'immorality'; if they were, they must have been a very different breed of people from the ones who now congregate in the basement preview theatres of Wardour Street. This does not mean, however, that their reactions were false: they were based on the public morality of the time and so reflected a sense of social responsibility. Reviewers, then as now, saw films outside the context of the public theatres, at press previews, but with an awareness of the effect that they would have on a wider audience.

What they perceived was a *deliberate* flouting of established codes: 'calculated vileness', 'calculated perversion', 'calculated malevolence'. The depiction of violence is an assault on the audience, the depiction of cruelty a form of sadism. Hence evil, the subject-matter of the films, is felt to have been transferred, via the atmosphere and treatment, to the film itself, in a way that does not happen with the violence of the (traditional) Western or the investigative detective story — of a kind that British studios were making in quite large numbers at the time. The films become 'malevolent', 'vile' and 'perverted', and these qualities are not only intensified, but actually proven by the technical skills of the film-makers: *Time* speaks of 'malevolent dexterity' in relation to *Le Salaire de la peur* and C. A. Lejeune, elsewhere in the review quoted earlier, describes *Les Diaboliques* as 'extremely clever and very horrid'. There were clearly particular features of these films that distinguished them from other stories about violence and wrongdoing.

Certainly, Clouzot respects the convention that the criminals should be unmasked by the detective in the last scene (another departure from the novel, where Boileau-Narcéjac allow them to get away with their crime). But this, too, appears contrived — a final *coup de théâtre*. What was upsetting was the amorality of the crimes, the depiction of 'a suspenseful but sordid slice of French life' (Whiteley) and a commonplace, modern environment where men and women are conscienceless, driven by their desires, with no reference to ethical standards. Above all, the reviewers perceived sexual undertones, some of which might escape a later audience accustomed to the open depiction of sex on screen: the passion of Ravinel for his mistress, Lucienne; his frustration with his frigid wife; and the lesbian bond between the submissive wife and the dominant mistress.

Where the non-genre cinema of the time portrays love, *film noir* shows desire. Its brief encounters do not end in noble renunciation, but in death. Murder does not bring out the best in anyone and those caught in the act of murder tend to show human nature in its least attractive light. A film like *Les Diaboliques* exhibits this behaviour for the purpose of giving pleasure, so perhaps the reviewers were justified in seeing the province of *film noir* as the Devil's work and attributing an element of malevolence to the skilful film-maker. This Devil is all the more persuasive when we are invited to side with him 'as one who perseveres in some purpose which he has conceived to be excellent' (Shelley, again, on *Paradise Lost*), and does so with a passion in contrast to the 'cold security of undoubted triumph' enjoyed by God (or, in *film noir*, by the Law). We know that crime will not pay, that the murderer will eventually be brought to justice. What moves us is the energy and ingenuity with which these *diaboliques* pursue their ends.

The Devil is also, etymologically, as Shelley reminds us, *diabolos*, 'an Accuser'. It is a role which we later shall see him adopt more specifically, though his indictment of human society and the fates that govern our lives is implicit in all *film noir*.

When films like *Le Salaire de la peur* and *Les Diaboliques* reached British and American audiences in the decade after the Second World War, they were seen as peculiarly 'French'. The American films of the 1940s which we classify as *films noirs* were the product of a rather different culture and historical moment. There is a broad overlap with gangster movies, and the underworld is frequently present in them, many of the protagonists being gangsters, mobsters or petty criminals, or else policemen, former policemen, detectives, private eyes, district attorneys or defence lawyers. There is a similar overlap with the investigative crime mystery: it is often the plot that requires a detective or private eye at the centre of the action, the role sometimes being taken by investigators for various federal agencies or insurance companies and, quite frequently, also by journalists and reporters. The local newspaper was a well-established feature of American life, both in large cities and small towns, and this made it a plausible starting-point for an enquiry. Traditionally the source of truth and a bastion against corruption, it was also (like the law) potentially tainted by its association with wrongdoing: the American crime reporter is not always a glamorous figure and the surroundings in which he works — newspaper office or mean streets — have a seediness which explains their ambivalent allure immediately after the war.

The historical moment also accounts for the fact that many of the protagonists of American *film noir* are war veterans, often scarred by their experiences or, at least, alienated from the cosy small-town environment to which they return. The settings of these films may often be superficially reassuring: communities like any in Middle America, ordinary neighbourhoods, the mansions of wealthy families; but the characters are just as often rootless, inhabiting dingy hotel rooms, night clubs and bars, even when they are not already underworld figures. And the small towns and neighbourhoods, on closer examination, turn out to be indeed any anonymous small town or neighbourhood, the families that inhabit the mansions are driven apart by greed and desire, with missing relatives often providing the impetus for the story. Women, who should be the focus of stability, are unhappy, frustrated or vindictive if married; and, if not, appear as singers, models, strippers and night-club hostesses, roles in which they can be plausibly shown as the victims of crime.

The 1940s were also the period during which Sigmund Freud began to penetrate the consciousness of Hollywood. Not surprisingly, disturbed individuals are often the perpetrators in films where the subject is murder; but the psychiatrist also becomes a recurrent figure, seen notably in Alfred Hitchcock's *Spellbound* (1945) where Gregory Peck and Ingrid Bergman are cast as members of the profession, and there is an attempt to portray the workings of the subconscious in an expressionist dream sequence designed by Salvador Dali. In this way, as well as the blackmailers and investigators required by the plot, the protagonists of American *films noirs* include many alcoholics, gamblers, psychotics and current or former mental patients, as well as a higher proportion of amnesiacs than one might expect to find in a typical subway carriage or bar.

The obvious element of contrivance in plots where a murder has been committed and the central character can't remember whether he did it or not, meant that it was easy to classify such films as 'just stories' and, especially for audiences outside the United States, to distance them from the real world. On the whole, British critics did not feel threatened by American *film noir*: one must remember that, in the 1940s and early 1950s, transatlantic society and culture were more distant than they have since become, and the image presented of them in these films intensified this: mobsters, psychiatrists, newsmen, federal investigators, private eyes and the streets of American cities had an exotic charm, but were a long way from the day-by-day experiences of life in postwar Europe. Even poverty in America belonged to a different order of poverty.

Continental films like those of Clouzot, on the other hand, were anchored in a more recognizable reality. Moreover, not being governed by the Hays Code, they could be more explicit about sexual motivations that had to remain implicit in Hollywood films: French lovers are clearly that and the figure of the prostitute (such as the one portrayed by Simone Signoret in Yves Allégret's *Dédée d'Anvers*, 1947, and elsewhere) is one of the most enduring in French cinema. The settings, too, are more varied and specific than those of American *film noir*: the Norman seaside town of Yves Allégret's *Une si jolie petite plage* (1948), the apartment blocks and boarding houses in Clouzot's films, the peasant milieu of Jacques Becker's *Goupi Mains Rouges* (1943). Most of all, the protagonists are people in everyday jobs, successors to the working-class heroes portrayed by Jean Gabin in the 1930s and serving the purpose of directors whose interest was not only to create suspense, but to observe the range of typical or eccentric characters in a given environment. The criminals in Georges Lacombe's *Leur dernière nuit* (1953), Gilles Grangier's *Reproduction interdite* (1956) or Léo Joannon's *L'Homme aux clés d'or* (1956) are not psychotics or mental patients, but a librarian, the owner of an art gallery and a student, like the school teacher of *Les Diaboliques*, the children of bourgeois parents in André Cayatte's *Avant le déluge* (1954) or the lawyer in Claude Autant-Lara's *En cas de malheur* (1958).

Crime, here, is not safely cordoned off in the underworld of the gangsters who feature so largely in American cinema: the milieu of these French films is not *the* Milieu, but an integral part of society; and the message is that expressed in the title of André Cayatte's *Nous sommes tous des assassins* (1952): we are all murderers, we are all implicated. The mechanics of the plot in *Les Diaboliques* were far-fetched: it was something else that made the film so disturbing to its first British critics. Their children would go to Saturday morning cinema shows where they could see more violent deaths in a thirty-minute Western than in the whole of *Les Diaboliques*. The difference that made the French film so 'malevolent' was the 'realism' of the setting and the intentions of the film-maker. Clouzot set out to shock both by Grand Guignol effects and by displaying the commonplace nature of evil, asking the audience to identify with the characters and then demonstrating that its imagination could be excited not only by the deed, but by the idea that precedes the deed. The appetite must be aroused before one sups with the Devil — and, in its closeness to everyday life, a film like *Les Diaboliques* seemed to offer too short a spoon.

II.

LA ROUTE DE VILLENNES

After midnight, on a lonely road outside Paris. Two cars, approaching from opposite directions, pull up with headlights blazing, and sound their horns. At this signal, the occupants get out, four from one car, three from the other, and with military precision one man leaves each group and starts to march briskly across the twenty or so metres that separate them. As they pass, exchanging a few words, we notice that they are both carrying submachine guns slung across their shoulders. However, like all those present, they are dressed in business suits.

The purpose of this meeting is an exchange, and the two armed men are there to convey what is being bartered from one group to the other: on one side, four suitcases full of gold bars; on the other, a prisoner, also smartly dressed, with a blindfold and his hands handcuffed behind his back. The exchange takes place, and the men who have taken the gold bars drive off, leaving the other three with the released prisoner, standing beside their car.

At this moment, they see a new set of headlights in the distance. 'I told you that I heard two cars,' the prisoner says. The four men dive for cover. They are only just in time: in fact, one does not manage to reach the safety of the ditch, but ducks behind the car. An open-topped car sweeps past and its occupants hurl hand grenades into the stationary vehicle, killing the man who was crouching behind it. As the smoke dies down, they turn, stop the car and walk over in line abreast to inspect the damage. There are three of them, all carrying revolvers, one very fat. There is a burst of gunfire from the ditch and the three fall grotesquely, a figure in a light-coloured suit sliding to the ground beside a notice that reads: *AUTOROUTE de l'OUEST à 1 km.*

During the whole of this time, there has been no sign of any other vehicle, still less of the police. It is only after a chase, and another shoot-out which leaves three more dead and a car blazing beside the road, that civilians threaten to make an appearance; they are introduced purely to round off the scene. The film, which is Jacques Becker's *Touchez pas au grisbi*, revolves around the struggle for possession of the gold bars, and is supposedly set in the Parisian underworld at the time when it was made (1954). The locations — the cafés and nightclubs of Montmartre, hotels and apartment buildings, the Villennes road where the shoot-out takes place — are identifiable and authentic. As the film moves towards the climax I have described, we may start to wonder: is this really France in the 1950s, this country where prisoners are brutally interrogated in cellars and rival gangs settle their differences with sten guns and hand grenades? Were the police under the Fourth Republic so ineffectual that they can be adequately represented by two men peddling along on bicycles? The only figures of properly constituted authority that we see are merely street furniture. Professional thieves take calculated risks; and, indeed, these men in their pin-stripes or Italian suits, who drive smart saloon cars and associate with attractive young women, have the manners of businessmen. Yet they waste one another like frontline troops. This is not crime, it is war.

However, if this is a war, it is not one between uniformed armies, but the war, only ten years earlier on these same locations in France, involving what Jean-Pierre Melville, in the title of his 1969 film, dubbed 'The Army in the Shadows' — *L'Armée des ombres*. The German Occupation cast doubt on the legitimacy of the State authorities. The French police had an ambiguous relationship with the occupier, as did some members of the underworld. According to Rui Nogueira's *Le Cinéma selon Melville*, the French (as opposed to the German) Gestapo was made up of both policemen and criminals: 'In the most celebrated Gestapo headquarters in Paris, in the Rue Lauriston, you could find both Abel Davos and Inspector Bory. The underworld never got over it.'

The southern part of the country was ruled from Vichy by the puppet government of Marshal Pétain. The Resistance was made up of communists, in cells that had already been driven into clandestinity by the time war broke out, catholics, Gaullists (who set out to unify the movement behind the Conseil National de la Résistance), intellectuals and independents, including some criminals: the underworld too, whichever side it chose to support, had the advantage of habits of concealment. Pre-war moral certainties disappeared: this was a time of rivalries and of betrayals, not always clearly motivated. What had previously been illegal might now be construed as legitimate, though still illegal in the eyes of the State. The loyalties and the morality of participants in a civil war are ambiguous.

This ambivalence is a source of ironies. It is a cruel irony, in *L'Armée des ombres*, that the Resistance heroine Mathilde, played by Simone Signoret, has to be executed by her own boss. When the two armed men, whose job it is to carry out the exchange of prisoner for bullion in *Touchez pas au grisbi*, cross at the halfway point between the cars, one says to the other: '*Tiens, Marco, bonsoir quand même*'. They are merely foot-soldiers, former associates, now placed by fate in opposite camps. Marco is shortly to be killed: he is the man who shelters behind the car. His opposite number must know that there is a second vehicle ready for this double-cross, but even so (*quand même*), he sees no reason for not saying hello. The moral ambiguities of a period that set Frenchman against Frenchman are evoked, too, in the forced glamour of the nightclub in Becker's film, where the ambiance is the same as in those places where German officers drank with French showgirls, and the collaborationist *beau monde* — the louche atmosphere of betrayal and immorality evoked in the novels of Patrick Modiano.

This is not to say that *Touchez pas au grisbi* is 'about' the Occupation. It is specifically not about that. It is about France in the 1950s, about a middle-aged criminal (Max-le-Menteur, played by Jean Gabin) who wants to retire after his last job, and is let down by a friend with a weakness for women. It is about the novel by Albert Simonin, which Becker adapted, and about the pleasure of audiences who are asked to sense, behind the familiar settings of Montmartre in the 1950s, another Montmartre where the underworld, *le milieu*, conducts its affairs unknown to *les caves*, the 'suckers', or ordinary, straight-living citizens. It is about the language of this *milieu*, an argot that made Simonin's reputation — he published a dictionary of it, which is essential for readers of his novels. From Simonin, cinemagoers learned to refer to a car as *une tire*, a million francs as *une brique*, a gun as *un flingue*, the cinema as *le cinoche*, and to say '*on me fait du suif*' when someone was causing them trouble. The film is about fictional worlds, including those portrayed by Warner Bros in the 1930s and 1940s. But its setting and language are French and it belongs to a country which had barely emerged from the German Occupation, so that too is a presence in the film and partly explains why the 'enemy' fights with stick grenades, of the type used by the Wehrmacht, and why the underworld settles its accounts in a context where there is no reference to the authority of the State.

Jacques Becker's first film, *Dernier atout* (1942), was made during the Occupation, but can be forgiven for saying nothing about contemporary events. It is set in 'Clarical, capital of an imaginary country' (apparently in Latin America), where two police cadets graduate with the same mark and have to solve a 'real' crime to decide which of them shall come top of the class. A murder conveniently takes place and the pair find themselves pursuing the killer of Tony Amanito, American Public Enemy Number One, *un crime de luxe*, according to one of them, since it has taken place not in a mere hotel, but *un palace*, with white telephones and ladies called 'Bella' and 'Pearls', who drive around in black limousines and wear hats that would not look out of place in the window of a pastry-shop.

'We thought that people deprived of American movies would doubtless like to see an adventure story with gangsters for heroes,' Becker said in an interview with Jacques Rivette and François Truffaut (for *Cahiers du cinéma*, issue 32, February 1954). He had been taken prisoner by the Germans early in the war and returned to Paris at the end of 1941 to find the city occupied and its cinema audiences cut off from the world's main supplier of popular entertainment. *Dernier atout*, with its exotic names (Gonzalès, Murphy, Mme Collins and a Chicago mobster called Rudy Score, played by Pierre Renoir) tried to fill the gap with a native version of the 1930s Hollywood thriller.

This is what makes it interesting. Technically, it is primitive compared to Becker's later works, like *Casque d'or* or *Touchez pas au grisbi* — if nothing else, contrast the unimaginative use of jazz and dance-band music, as an insistent background on the soundtrack of *Dernier atout*, with the haunting repetition of 'Max's tune' in *Grisbi*. But as a product designed to supply a need for American-style thrillers, it highlights what Becker and his co-writers (Maurice Aubergé, Louis Chavance and Maurice Griffe) thought characteristic of these Hollywood films.

The opulent 'white telephone' settings are one thing, the refusal to take them seriously, another. More significant than these, however, are the personalities and behaviour of the two rival detectives. They fit effortlessly into the surroundings where the crime was committed, and are experts at the throwaway line. While Pierre Renoir, as Rudy, exudes an air of polite menace, the young detective Clarence (Raymond Rouleau) never loses his cool, even when captured by Rudy, and he charms the gangster's moll (Mireille Balin) — who, predictably, turns out to be quite a good sort before the final credits.

'*Vous n'êtes pas bête*', Score tells Clarence: in fact there are repeated references to one or other of the young detectives being 'no fool'. They show their wits principally in exchanges with the two women in the case (Balin and Catherine Cayret), both of whom are involved with crooks. Wisecracking; the ability to keep one's cool and nonchalantly light up a cigarette when a villain is threatening to have one of his henchmen blow out your brains; above all, the ability to deal effectively with women, the more subtly dangerous sex, whose allure is enhanced by wealth, especially when there is a suggestion that it might have been immorally gained: this is the character of the hero, American-style.

'Why should those on the right side of the law be less tough than bandits?' the police chief asks at the end of the film, when his subordinate pays tribute to Clarence's resilience. Indeed, the heroes are in the end tougher, and smarter, than the villains, but their methods vary little if at all: respect is what they demand from the villains, so Score's appreciation of Clarence's wit is one we are expected to share. Toughness and wit (in other words, physical and intellectual power), are what attracts the heroines, which explains their tendency to hang around with the criminal classes and to reveal their better natures only when someone like Clarence arrives to chat them up. Underneath, this amorality of the women in such films has to do, partly, with censorship: the gangster's moll is no virgin, but a 'sophisticated' woman, who could be understood in Hollywood movies to do things with our hero that the Hays Code would not allow her to talk about, let alone get up to, on screen. Censors in France had always worked to a more relaxed code (in *Grisbi*, Max's English mistress can be shown unambiguously in bed), but a Hollywood-style film had to adopt a particular version of the sex war that involved suave men with women whose sexual availability was signalled by their lack of moral sense in other directions: women fallen among thieves, with questionable backgrounds, needing the right tough guy to reveal their better qualities.

Grisbi, as Colette Audry pointed out on its release (*Les Temps modernes*, November 1954), differs from earlier films in the genre because its hero, while ready to sacrifice everything for his friend, prefers sleep to sex. A middle-aged hero too tired to accept the offer of a night with Jeanne Moreau was certainly a novelty; and when his English mistress calls out from the bedroom: '*Tu m'aimes, Max?*', he stubs out his cigarette and says 'Coming', in a voice that is not coolly dispassionate, just faintly bored. Of course, Max does get the offers; but he is ready for an armistice in this war, as in the other.

The period of the Occupation itself, despite its potential as a source of plots and its influence on the postwar mood, was the setting for only a few thrillers: André Berthomieu's *Peleton d'exécution* (1945), for example, and Maurice de Canonge's *Mission spéciale* (1946). Raymond Bernard's *Un Ami viendra ce soir* (1946) was set in a lunatic asylum, where some of the inmates are genuinely mad, and others members of the Resistance who use the place as a cover for their activities — a nice metaphor for the deceptions of the time. But, in the main, the genre film was founded on a premise — escapism — which precluded reference to such recent, and painful, events. This may partly explain the failure to make a series based on the character of the detective Nestor Burma, created by the leading French writer of 'hardboiled' thrillers, Léo Malet. Jacques Daniel-Norman's film *120 rue de la Gare* (1945), adapted from Malet's work, is situated during the Occupation, with René Dary playing the private eye; but there were no sequels. The usual explanation for this is Dary's height: he was so short that he had to stand on a stool to measure up to his leading lady, Sophie Desmarets, and refused to play opposite her again. There was probably only room for one serial private eye in French cinema, and Eddie Constantine, as Lemmy Caution, took over. Malet later remarked wryly that if Dary had been taller, Constantine would not have ended as the owner of a racing stables.

If one successor to *Grisbi* is *L'Armée des ombres* (which even critics accused of being more thriller than war film), the successors to the Clarence of *Dernier atout* are the characters that Raymond Rouleau went on to play in André Hunebelle's films *Mission à Tanger* (1949), *Méfiez-vous des blondes* (1950) and *Massacre en dentelles* (1951); and Lemmy Caution. The series started in 1953 with *La Môme vert-de-gris*, and was rapidly followed by *Cet homme est dangereux* (1953), *Les Femmes s'en balancent* (1954), *Ça va barder* (1954) and *Je suis un sentimental* (1955); the character, as an emblem of 1950s cinema, was later revived by Jean-Luc Godard in *Alphaville* (1965). The original films had the cachet of Anglo-Saxon source material in the novels by Peter Cheyney, and an authentic American star. At a time when French critics, like those of *Cahiers du cinéma*, were beginning to recognize the qualities of American *film noir* — with such enthusiasm that their gift of a genre label stuck and was universally adopted — French audiences got a naturalized version of the hard-boiled thriller in the adventures of Lemmy, roving agent for the FBI, whose work (if not done in the studios) tended to take him to European locations within easy reach, where he could speak French, though with a pleasing American drawl.

It was not the French of Racine, neither was it quite that of Simonin: a simplified version of the underworld slang in *Grisbi*, and less inventive. Lemmy spent his time, off-duty and on, in nightclubs, country houses and casinos, travelling between these locations in the open-topped 1950s cars now much prized by collectors: it was not the cars, but the locations that lacked the specific character of the Montmartre settings in *Grisbi*. Lemmy's personality was equally bland. Every film found him involved in some mess that he would describe as *une salade*. Always immaculately dressed, ready with his fists, he liked gambling, elegant women (addressed as '*mon sucre*', '*p'tite soeur*' or '*mon trésor*') and, above all, whisky. 'Time for my medicine,' he would say, pouring another glass. Forty years on, instead of the cool cat that he so obviously thinks himself, he seems strictly neanderthal: apart from his vulgar brawling, his sexism appears gross and his alcoholism suicidal.

To say that, however, is to ignore the self-mockery that is the most memorable quality of the films. '*Encore une salade*,' Lemmy says, direct to camera, as things start to hot up for the nth time in *Les Femmes s'en balancent*. '*Je suis un tendre*,' he remarks in the same film, mocking his tough image and anticipating the title of *Je suis un sentimental*. Sentimental, he wasn't, and the humour would have been introduced by an intelligent star — who could hardly have played such a part without at least a hint of self-mockery — even if it had not been in the scripts. The series exploits the conventions of the genre, with a knowing wink to the audience, most of whom must have been aware that there was a measure of self-referential irony. You might say that they are post-modernist, before post-modernism — which makes them only slightly less silly as films.

It takes two or more works to constitute a genre — usually many more — and, consequently, no individual work except the first can acquire its right of entry to the group without reference to its fellow-members. In other words, a thriller exists as a thriller, not *de facto*, but because there are other thrillers to which it can be related in plot, style, theme, characters or structure. And, in the case of a cinema genre, this network of relationships becomes still more complex, because in addition to other films, the *film noir*, *film policier*, gangster movie, murder story, thriller or courtroom drama are also linked by subject-matter and ethos to literary works of the same genre, from which they are often adapted, as well as to 'real life' — here meaning the crime stories in newspapers — which cinema evokes in a peculiarly concrete way through the depiction of visible events in what are often actual locations, or studio sets designed to suggest them.

The climax of Jacques Becker's film *Touchez pas au grisbi*, the shoot-out on the Villennes road, seemed a good point at which to start this investigation, because it is an excellent film and one that most people would agree is a typically French example of the genre — in a way that *Dernier atout* and the Lemmy Caution movies are not. This is not, however, because Montmartre in the early 1950s was really inhabited by gangsters armed with automatic weapons and hand grenades. What makes the film 'French' is nothing so simple as a direct relationship with the realities of Parisian life in its time.

The 'Frenchness' does have to do with the settings, of course: Becker is not striving, as he did in *Dernier atout*, to find an exotic context for the action but, on the contrary, to suggest that his 'underworld' exists just below the surface of everyday life. The entrance to this underworld is protected from *les caves*, the outsiders, who do not belong there, by a Cerberus of social and linguistic conventions that *les caves* do not share. At the start of the film, three of these outsiders try to get a table in Bouche's restaurant. Bouche politely turns them away, saying that she is fully booked, and that they will do very well across the road at Victor's. '*Merde, alors,* they don't have a clue what's going on this year, *les caves,*' remarks one of the girls at Max's table, as the little group of ordinary citizens goes off and Bouche starts to lower the shutters on the restaurant door. We, as the audience, are privileged to remain.

Paris, like every European capital, has a social geography that dates back to the Middle Ages: scholarship in the Quartier Latin, the Church on the Ile de la Cité and commerce around Les Halles, with the palace of the Louvre being added in the sixteenth century on the site of the medieval castle. During the nineteenth century, this social geography had been given dramatic colour in the novels of Balzac and Zola; Balzac's *César Birotteau*, for example, making a sharp distinction between the high-class suppliers of luxury goods at the end of the Rue Saint-Honoré that adjoins the Tuileries Gardens, and the wholesale traders at the other where the thoroughfare meets the warren of little streets round Les Halles, both being contrasted with the rich banking quarter to the North. Zola, in *Le Ventre de Paris* and *Au Bonheur des Dames*, analyzed the market of Les Halles and the life of a department store with the rigour of a sociologist, the titles of other Parisian novels in his series *Les Rougon-Macquart* giving equally clear indications of their subject-matter: *L'Argent* (the stock exchange), *L'Assomoir* (the working-class gin palace), *L'Oeuvre* (the artist's life). Marcel Proust, Jules Romains and numerous other twentieth-century novelists contributed further fictional highlights to the map of the city.

'In the daytime, [the district] offers nothing of interest', the Michelin Guide of the 1950s said of the area around the Boulevard de Clichy — so its readers knew what to expect. In the years after the Liberation, the nightclubs of Pigalle turned from entertaining the foreign occupier to entertaining the foreign tourist. Other quarters were devoted to bourgeois family life (the sixteenth *arrondissement*, for example), intellectual pursuits, commerce, industry, administration and government, according to a division between various forms of work and play that was pleasing to the puritanical bourgeois mind. However, in Pigalle business and pleasure were dangerously combined. Here was wealth without class, glamour without taste or art, and exploitation without the whitewash of respectability.

At ten o'clock in the morning, you could walk away from the market of Les Halles, where the traders were clearing up after their night's work, towards Montmartre along the Boulevard Sébastopol and see a few prostitutes already jangling their doorkeys. In the evening, in the Rue Saint-Denis, which runs parallel to the Boulevard Sébastopol, the street would be lined on both sides with women waiting for clients. In Pigalle itself, music halls, nightclubs and strip joints came to life when the theatres closed and did not shut down until dawn, offering pleasures that the Michelin Guide leaves its readers largely to discover for themselves, if they care to pause on their walk towards the Basilica in Montmartre. Everyone could see the outward signs of the area's main industries and guess how the money here was made and spent. As American *film noir* was to explore locations in Los Angeles, San Francisco and New York (but is just as often set against a generalized, anonymous urban background), French cinema in the 1950s exploits the romance of Pigalle, celebrated in dozens of films like Léo Joannon's *Le Désert de Pigalle* (1957), Georges Lacombe's white slave trade thriller, *Cargaison blanche* (1957) and Mario Landi's *Maigret à Pigalle*, as well as in the work of Meville, Becker and Dassin.

In the parallel world of cinema, Gabin, Moreau and Lino Ventura became familiar inhabitants of these locations. Their authenticity was also confirmed, both before and after *Touchez pas au grisbi*, by the fact that none of them has worked for long periods abroad. For foreign audiences, in 1954, the film's relatively uninhibited attitude to sexual relationships identified it as 'a Continental movie', as opposed to an American one. It is not only that the characters are shown to have sexual relationships without the formality of marriage or even much love, but also that sex is not especially important. It matters to Riton and is the cause of his downfall, as Max suspects it will be from the start, wryly remarking that his friend is too old to make a fool of himself over a woman. Max, you might say, then goes on to make a fool of himself over Riton, but with no illusions about what he is doing.

The friendship between Max and Riton, around which the narrative of the film revolves, derives from a perennial theme in French cinema which goes back at least to the era of the

Popular Front: Gabin played in Julien Duvivier's *La Belle équipe* (1936), the film that best evokes the comradeship of the Popular Front era, before going on to make his name as the doomed hero of those Marcel Carné/Jacques Prévert films of the last 1930s, the ordinary soldier in Jean Renoir's *La Grande illusion* (1937) and the working man in Renoir's *La Bête humaine* (1938). He brought elements of all these pre-war, non-gangster parts to Max: loyalty, pessimism, tenderness and a sense of the ironies of fate.

The contrary of comradeship is enmity, and of loyalty, betrayal. I suggested that *Touchez pas au grisbi* is a war film, because of the weaponry deployed on the Villennes road and the marked absence of any higher authority like the police: war is criminal activity licensed by circumstances and unconstrained by notions of legality. *Grisbi* is not a detective story that uncovers the perpetrator of a crime, or a cops-and-robbers story that puts us on the side of the law against the villains, but a story of conflict between rivals outside the law that invites us to support Max's values (fidelity to Riton) against those of Angelo (betrayal of his former friends). Its ethos, as well as its hardware, is that of the war movie where comradeship and loyalty are what counts.

At the same time, it belongs aesthetically to the genre of the Warner Bros gangster movies of the 1930s and 1940s, just as *Dernier atout* and the Lemmy Caution films belong to an American genre of hardboiled 1930s detective thrillers (including comedy thrillers like *The Thin Man*). But where the Lemmie Caution series succeeded only in translating the styles of their American originals, implausibly, into a French context, *Grisbi* managed to naturalize the equally foreign world of the Chicago mobster and to make it plausible in a Montmartre which certainly housed criminals, even criminal gangs, but did not in reality experience the sort of wholesale and uncontrolled violence depicted in the film. It was able to do so because it was made at a time when it could call on fresh memories of the Occupation, divided loyalties, street fights and the underground Resistance.

This is what makes Becker's film a peculiarly French thriller, which can serve as a point of reference to study the genre before and after the mid-1950s. We can understand that it belongs to the same context as Jules Dassin's suspense thriller, *Du rififi chez les hommes* (1955), and that the theme of male comradeship had been developed, as we have seen, in Clouzot's *Le Salaire de la peur* (1953). In 1955, Jean-Pierre Melville, who had been a *résistant* in Paris and discovered the reality of the underworld through its ambiguous contacts with the Resistance movements and the Gestapo, made *Bob le Flambeur*, another ironic story about a scam that goes wrong, and in 1960 *Le Trou*, about the betrayal of a prison escape. The peculiar circumstances of the war in France justified the sense of malevolent fate that, in the pre-war movies of Carné and Prévert, had seemed more of a pose, motivated by nothing except a faintly adolescent pessimism and disgust with the world.

The Villennes road leads back, then, to the road taken by the two reconciled friends, Emile and Louis, at the end of René Clair's *A nous la liberté* (1931), via the desperate road driven by the expatriates in *Le Salaire de la peur*; and forward to the roads followed by the outsiders of the New Wave in *A bout de souffle* (1960) and *Pierrot le Fou* (1965). On it, men (sometimes accompanied by women) confront questions of freedom, loyalty, courage, escape, money, desire and the ironies of fate. There is no sign along the way of the *police routière*: The morality of the French gangster film of the 1950s is not one of cops versus robbers and its search for the truth does not begin with the question: whodunnit? Where the investigative thriller begins in darkness and sets out to cast light, *Touchez pas au grisbi* reaches its climax past midnight on the Villennes road, with a blazing car and the destruction of everything that Angelo has fought to gain and Max to preserve. This is a view of the human condition that does not take as its starting-point a belief in the triumph of justice and truth.

Gabin was not the only actor whom Becker considered for

the rôle of Max: his first and second choices were Daniel Gélin and François Périer. For Riton, he got René Dary and for the nightclub owner, Pierrot, Paul Francoeur. Finally, to play Angelo, he picked a newcomer, Lino Ventura, a former wrestler who went on to play the tough guy in many later crime movies and the Resistance hero/narrator in *L'Armée des ombres*: Becker and Melville allegedly spotted him wrestling at the Salle Wagram. *Touchez pas au grisbi* was an immediate success, with 250,000 admissions in Paris before general release. In genre fiction, one success creates others: as well as *Du rififi chez les hommes* and *Bob le Flambeur*, *Grisbi* was followed in 1955 by Henri Decoin's *Razzia sur le chnouf* (with Gabin, from a novel by Auguste Le Breton), Gilles Grangier's *Gas-Oil* (again with Gabin, as a lorry driver against the Mafia); in 1956 by Pierre Billon's *Jusqu'au dernier*; in 1957 by Grangier's *Le Rouge est mis* (novel and script by Le Breton) and Alain Delon's first film, Yves Allégret's *Quand la femme s'en mèle*; and in 1958 by Bernard Borderie's *Le Gorille vous salue bien*, adapted from a series of secret-agent novels by Antoine Dominique, with Ventura for the first time playing what was to become one of his best-known roles.

After being brought together by Becker, Ventura and Gabin became friends and met again in Henri Verneuil's *Le Clan des siciliens* (1969) — a film of much the same type as *Touchez pas au grisbi*, adapted from a novel by Le Breton (who, with Simonin, was the main writer of gangster fiction for the *Série Noire*). Jeanne Moreau, in the years before the New Wave, made several films in which she played the mistress of criminals or gangsters, notably Louis Malle's first film, *Ascenseur pour l'échafaud* (1958). But, as Malle points out in his conversations with Philip French, *Malle on Malle* , the role was a departure for Moreau (invented for the film, because there was no leading female character in the novel by Noël Calef), casting her as the woman in an adulterous affair in which the two lovers hardly meet. The telephone is their only means of communication, and one that underlines their isolation.

The war, here, is a different one. The plot is a B-movie story about a man (Maurice Ronet) who is having an affair with his boss's wife (Moreau); so, together, they decide to kill him. The perfect locked-door murder is foiled by a typical Parisian concierge in the office block where it takes place, who turns off the electricity for the weekend and leaves Ronet stuck in the lift. Meanwhile his sports car is stolen by a young working-class man who wants to show off to his girlfriend, finds Ronet's gun in the glove compartment and commits the unplanned murder of a German tourist in a motel off the autoroute: since the young man panics and allows the gun to be found, it is easily traced back to Ronet, who walks out of the lift into the arms of the police.

This is so contrived that I make no apologies for giving away the ending: the interest of the film is elsewhere. The narrative obviously combines elements of traditional detective fiction, notably James M. Cain's *The Postman Always Rings Twice* (for the irony of the killer being caught for the wrong crime). Malle abandons the 'Vieux Paris' of Becker's Montmartre and instead gets his photographer Henri Decaë to explore the Nouveau Paris with its modern office buildings, motorways and motels. The central character belongs to this efficient new Paris as surely as Max to Montmartre: an ex-paratrooper, he plots his crime with military efficiency.

When the concierge respectfully addresses Ronet by his military title, Ronet brusquely reprimands him: we are civilians now. The New France has to be done with colonial wars and start looking towards the future — significantly, Ronet's boss is engaged in a deal in Algeria, still a French colony and fighting the war for independence that lasted until 1962. The year in which the film was made (1958) was the year in which the Fourth Republic fell and General de Gaulle came to power, proclaiming the end of inefficient coalition governments; and it was de Gaulle who made peace in Algeria and presided over the process of decolonization. By accident as much as by design, the film is an allegory for the moment, though it ends ironically with the forces of modernization foiled by a concierge with a game leg and a young tearaway who has ambitions, but no money, and none of the central figure's intelligence or strength of character.

The influence of Hitchcock may be taken for granted, but another, more immediate source is an outstanding French suspense film, Robert Bresson's *Un condamné à mort s'est échappé* (1956), on which Malle had worked as cameraman: the audience could hardly fail to think of the earlier movie in the scenes where Ronet is patiently observed escaping from the jammed lift. If you wished to classify *Un condamné à mort s'est échappé*, you would have to describe it as a prison escape movie, owing something to First and Second World War POW literature and movies, and giving much to *Escape from Alcatraz* (1979), which was clearly inspired by it. Bresson's film is certainly a suspense movie, though it is not a crime thriller. But, apart from Bresson's Catholicism which makes the film the story also of a spiritual journey, there is a small but significant difference between this and either POW movies or prison escapes. The prisoner in *Un condamné à mort s'est échappé*, though governed by no Geneva convention, represents the forces of legitimacy and his captors those of illegality. Ultimately, the morality of the escape can only be judged by reference to individual conscience and the legitimacy of the Resistance: it is the product of historical circumstances with no precise parallel in American history, but many in the recent history of Europe.

Perhaps the most 'American' element of all in *Ascenseur pour l'échafaud* is Jeanne Moreau who was already an established star by the end of the 1950s. She denies that she had become typecast in the role of a prostitute, and she had certainly played a variety of parts, including the girlfriend of a character in *Touchez pas au grisbi*; she forms a link between the well-crafted genre cinema of the 1950s and the New Wave. But an intelligent expression and slightly creaking voice gave her an air of worldly wisdom that made her difficult to cast as an *ingénue*, so she was tending to become a kind of French counterpart of Barbara Stanwyck — the *femme fatale* or showgirl, rather than the innocent young thing. 'At the start,' she told me, when I interviewed her in London in 1993, 'I worked with the sort of directors that François Truffaut wrote devastating things about when he was a critic; but they taught me so much — they taught me what I disliked. All the directors I worked with taught me, not only about my craft, but about life.' She was also a veteran stage actress, who had played with the Comédie Française and opposite Gérard Philipe in the Théâtre National Populaire.

When Malle asked her to take a part in his first film, she brought this experience with her, and he acknowledges that she was 'incredibly helpful' in teaching him about working with actors. Characteristically, she repays the compliment, saying that he taught her a good deal about cinema: 'film-making is an exchange'. She also met Malle's scriptwriter, the right-wing novelist Roger Nimier, whom she liked immediately, 'because he was outrageous... He was involved in politics at a period when it was a sort of romantic attitude' — a romanticism of the right that is evident in the character played by Maurice Ronet, individualistic, resourceful, contemptuous of bourgeois conformism. Many 'heroes' of classic *film noir* (who are, in conventional terms, villains) seem to be trying to escape from an over-regulated society towards more primitive times; their rule is the survival of the fittest (and, consequently, the elimination of the unfit); and it is not only the left that despises the bourgeoisie. In this sense, *film noir* may become a sort of urban Western, with an underlying nostalgia for a mythical past. Ronet, in *Ascenseur pour l'échafaud*, is applying the simple morality that he has learned in the jungles of Indochina to the concrete jungle of contemporary Paris, and his defeat by fate can almost be seen as tragic, as well as just.

The notion of a particular genre is a model, a sort of Platonic 'idea', of which any individual work is the more or less 'impure' translation into the concrete form of book, film, etc. Even the first example, only recognized as such when it has been followed by others, appears retrospectively as a tentative excursion into territory that becomes more clearly delineated by later explorers. Moreover, in the particular field that concerns us, that of crime stories, there is no single concept of the boundaries, but a core notion around which it is possible to group a number of satellite notions, or sub-genres: detective stories, murder stories, *films noirs*, *films policiers*, gangster films, courtroom dramas and thrillers, possibly combining elements of horror film, war film, espionage and political thrillers, psychological dramas or social problem films; or serving as a model for any narrative that involves investigation of a mystery, allegories of business and politics, concepts of legality; and drawing inspiration or source material from literature, actuality, history, comic strips or other films.

Following one line, that of 'aesthetic context', we can understand Jacques Becker's film *Touchez pas au grisbi* and Louis Malle's film *Ascenseur pour l'échafaud* as works derived from literary originals (the novels by Albert Simonin and Noël Calef) which in turn derived from American popular entertainment in pulp fiction or cinema. These also contribute certain themes, like the irony of fate, that were strongly evident in French cinema before the Second World War, and supply some of the intellectual enjoyment that the audience derives from the films. One of the main pleasures of genre fiction is this dissimilarity to everyday reality that comes from the closure of the narrative: there is a plot, with a precise beginning and a neatly-rounded end. An arrest, a death or simply the playing of 'Max's tune' after Max has learned of the death of Riton and the failure of his plans, gives a sense of completion that one seldom enjoys in real life. Constructing such a narrative, with no loose ends, is a skill learned by example.

Yet there is also a social context to both films: the Montmartre underworld in *Touchez pas au grisbi*, the environment created by post-war modernization in *Ascenseur pour l'échafaud*; and a historical context, more obliquely evoked: the Occupation of the 1940s in one, and the colonial wars of the 1950s in the other. The fact that films ostensibly made for ends of pure entertainment could incorporate such references — and, perhaps, could not avoid doing so — was in itself an object lesson. French critics from the early 1950s had discovered the truth of what audiences had long believed: that American thrillers, like American westerns, however contrived and commercial, accurately portrayed certain aspects of American society, if only because a society also describes itself through its myths.

The processes of modernization and decolonization in France, explicitly mentioned in *Ascenseur pour l'échafaud*, were to provide the context for a shift in emphasis in French thrillers during the next decade. General de Gaulle was brought to power by the Army, on the understanding that he would keep Algeria French, and one outcome of the Evian Agreements (as a result of which Algeria eventually became independent) was the creation of the terrorist *Organisation Armée Secrète*. The government believed that this form of terrorism could only be defeated through the creation of underground, counter-terrorist units of 'parallel police'. In 1961, the word *barbouze* entered the language to describe these government secret agents (with their 'false beards'), who acted on behalf of the authorities, but outside the law and, people came to suspect, beyond its control.

Here was a possible source of narratives that fitted well into the context of existing genre cinema, with the themes of ambiguous or divided loyalties and the legitimacy of state power that were already implied in *Touchez pas au grisbi*. By the mid-1960s, directors and scriptwriters were fully aware of ways in which the conventions and structures of genre fiction could serve as a vehicle and a cover for political comment. But, then, perhaps, they had always, consciously or unconsciously, served such ends. Like the pure model or Platonic 'idea' of the genre, the pure example of a *film policier*, innocent of any ulterior motive, immune to interpretation as anything except itself, might exist only as a theoretical construct. Just as the first example of a genre cannot become an example until there are others with which to compare it (and which, consequently, reveal its previously undetected nature as 'thriller', 'detective story', or whatever), so these later exploitations of the genre, by uncovering its capacity to serve a variety of ends, performed a critical function and revealed previously undetected motifs and impurities in their predecessors, like Freudian psychoanalysts unmasking the unconscious sexuality beneath the innocent games of a child.

III.

JAZZ

The French 'Poetic Realism' of the 1930s, sometimes called 'Popular Realism', co-existed with genre that might be described as 'Popular Unrealism' — the films of René Clair, the films in which Maurice Chevalier would break into song at the toss of a boater, and working-class heroes sang as they cycled along country lanes. Indeed, Chevalier and Gabin, Albert Préjean and Michel Simon, Fernandel and Arletty, Suzy Delair and Viviane Romance started their careers in music hall, though they would not necessarily appear as 'singing stars' on film. During the 1950s, Yves Montand pursued parallel careers as a singer and actor, playing dramatic roles in the cinema as well as making time for a *tour de chant* at the Olympia, in the Boulevard des Capucines, where he would interpret a typically French, bitter-sweet repertoire of humorous, sentimental and satirical songs.

The music of the Carné-Prévert films, as well as those made by René Clair, is the music of the orchestra, sometimes the guitar or the accordeon, perhaps justified by someone playing on screen. Jean Alfaro's score for Le *Dernier atout* is heavily romantic, Georges Auric's for *Le Salaire de la peur* has appropriately South American overtones. The background music of Jean Wiener in *Touchez pas au grisbi* makes a major contribution to the darkness of the movie, linking to the action through Max's theme, the air (played on the harmonica by Jean Wetzel), which the central character runs on the jukebox or which we hear at crucial moments as background. The sound style of all these films is as distinctive as their visual style — and at least as distinctively 'French'.

The use of Miles Davis's score for *Ascenseur pour l'échafaud* signals a quite different message. Jazz had featured in earlier films: in Curtis Bernhardt's *Carrefour* (1938) there is a scene with a black singer and an American band, for example, and Josephine Baker had naturalized jazz in the Parisian night club, so that such episodes were not out of place. But jazz came to stand for something different in the post-war world, something more emphatically American and 'foreign', as well as a constituent of the altogether French, pseudo-existentialist culture of Saint-German-des-Prés. Boris Vian, trumpet-player and author (as 'Vernon Sullivan') of the fake American thriller *J'irai cracher sur vos tombes*, was the most original figure in this interesting milieu, which the press linked both to the left-wing existentialism of Sartre and the nihilism of André Gide's *Les Caves du Vatican*. Fifties youth, in this caricature, was supposed to spend its nights in *caves*, listening to American music and the songs of Juliette Gréco, and its days in a state of passive existential despair or engaged in *actes* (probably *crimes*) *gratuits*. The rich *fils de papa* who hitched on to the poor students and intellectuals of Saint-Germain, and were distinguished from them by the fact that they had the keys to Papa's convertible, were those Marcel Carné tried unsuccessfully to describe in his morality tale, *Les Tricheurs* (titled 'Youthful Sinners' for export to the Anglo-Saxon world).

Underlying the bourgeois ethos of that film was a belief in

the 'immorality' of the post-war generation. The media stereotype implied that *ennui* was the cause, existentialism the philosophical justification and frenzied dancing the preamble for uninhibited sex. In the 1950s, Brigitte Bardot arrived on the scene and, at the end of the decade, married Jacques Charrier, star of *Les Tricheurs*. The precocious Françoise Sagan wrote *Bonjour Tristesse*, a novel of disillusionment born of a knowledge of life that seemed inappropriate for a 20-year old girl and set against a background of divorce, fast cars and holidays on the Côte. The impulsive killer in *Ascenseur pour l'échafaud* who, with his girlfriend from the flower shop, steals Maurice Ronet's American sports car, is a working-class youth who envies the lifestyle of the *fils de papa* and ends up committing a crime that is more or less *gratuit*: he has been led astray by the movies.

At least, that is a reading suggested by the conventional morality of the time; but Miles Davis tells us otherwise. For the generation to which Louis Malle belonged, the use of American jazz signalled rejection of the ethos (and the films) of the era to which Carné belonged. We are not expected to draw any moral lessons from *Ascenseur pour l'échafaud*, but to surrender to its depiction of the new France, of motorways and glass-fronted buildings, motels and sharp suits, still shackled with antiquated lifts and their dozy attendants. What is wrong with the working-class killer is not that he kills, but that he is so incompetent about it. His outlook is that of the old *régime*: accordeons, not Miles Davis.

Michel (Jean-Paul Belmondo), in Jean-Luc Godard's *A bout de souffle* (1960), could be his first cousin: 'look at the house where I was born,' he tells his American girlfriend (Jean Seberg), pointing to a typical Parisian apartment block. 'They've built a repulsive house across the road' — a concrete example of the new Paris. Indeed, his actions at the start of the film precisely mirror those of the young man in *Ascenseur pour l'échafaud*: he steals a car, finds a gun in the glove compartment and, on the spur of the moment, commits a murder. Michel (*'maintenant je fonce, Alphonse'*), with his cigarette, his hat, his gestures borrowed from Humphrey Bogart and his laid-back style, is yet another tearaway who has seen too many B-movies.

But where is Miles Davis? The music of Godard's film is a collage of sounds: violins, jazz, rock-and-roll, a Mozart clarinet concerto. The references to American culture are not implicit, but intrusive: the dedication to Monogram Pictures, the Lucky Strikes and Chesterfields that Patricia (Seberg) smokes, the couple's visit to a dubbed Western, Patricia's job selling *The International Herald Tribune.* 'Do you know William Faulkner?' she asks him, in the first of those rambling conversations about life and ideas that were to become one hallmark of the Godard *oeuvre.* 'No, who's that? Have you slept with him?' he answers, not having yet seen enough Godard movies to grasp what these conversations are meant to be about.

There are references, too, to the war, to the underworld, to the Gabin heroes with their hopeless longing for escape. Michel keeps talking about Italy and, specifically, of Cinecittà, where he pretends to have been offered some bit parts — in Neo-Realist films? *Ascenseur pour l'échafaud,* held together by its neatly rounded, ironic, improbable plot, consistent and motivated characters — and the music of Miles Davis — was a 'well-made film'. There is no such closure in *A bout de souffle.*

In the end, Patricia betrays him to the police, though for reasons that he, rightly, dismisses as reasonless. 'Regrets are stupid,' he tells her, in the conversation on Faulkner. 'I choose nothingness' (answering her implied question: 'I'd like to know what there is behind your face'). These are not real people, but characters in a film, who act the parts of gangster and moll because these are the ones they have been assigned by fate, or by the director. In the final scene, closing his own dying eyes, he mutters: 'You're really disgusting (*dégeulasse*).' She turns to the policeman to find out what he said. 'What does that mean, *dégeulasse?*' she asks, ending the film on a note of non-communication and remaining unmoved by its final ironic twist.

A bout de souffle owes something to François Truffaut (who suggested the idea), to Claude Chabrol and to Godard's cameraman, Raoul Coutard. It was the most distinctive of the early New Wave movies and full of references to the B-movies that the writers of *Cahiers du cinéma* liked. But these movies were not necessarily, or exclusively, *films noirs* and, considering Godard's film as supposedly a homage to that genre, one is immediately struck by what he has left out. The narrative, the location filming and the ironies may bear some resemblance to American models of the 1940s; but there is none of the expressionist visual style or the paranoia. Instead of taking place in rainy, windswept streets, *A bout de souffle* is filmed (except for a short section towards the end) in the broad sunlight of a Parisian summer. The locations are urban, but unthreatening: cafés, quite pleasant hotel rooms and whitewashed interiors. Far from repressing their sexuality (for it to emerge in odd camera angles, bouts of amnesia, Freudian dreams or dark passions), the couple speak openly about their desire for one another and about how many other partners they have had.

The most convincing tribute to American *film noir* was not made by any director of the New Wave, but one from that older generation which they were inclined, in general, to despise. Jean-Pierre Melville, as it happens, was one of the few Frenchmen associated with that earlier period to enjoy the approval of *Cahiers du cinéma*: in fact, Godard gave him a cameo acting role in *A bout de souffle*, as the author whom Jean Seberg goes to interview.

His 1959 film, *Deux hommes dans Manhattan*, is so close to a 1940s American B-movie that it verges on caricature: one is tempted to dismiss it as merely a less self-parodying successor to the Lemmy Caution series, and one which failed to achieve either critical or popular success. It is not a murder story: rather as Chabrol, in *Le Beau Serge* (1958) lifts a Hitchcockian motif (transfer of guilt) to take it outside the genre of the Hitchcockian thriller, so Melville uses the visual language (and some narrative elements) of *film noir* in what is not, strictly speaking, a *film noir* subject. A French diplomat at the United Nations has disappeared and a journalist from the Agence France-Presse bureau in New York (played by Melville) is sent to find him. He enlists the help of a photographer (Pierre Grasset) who works for '*France-Match*', and they follow the diplomat's trail from a series of photographs showing him with different women, only to discover at last that he died of a heart attack in the apartment belonging to his mistress. As he had been a Resistance hero, tortured by the Gestapo, the journalists face a moral dilemma: the photographer is quite prepared to smear the man's reputation by publishing his pictures of the dead body, while his friend and the boss of AFP try to persuade him that the circumstances should be covered up. 'Are you as cynical as you appear?' the AFP boss asks; and, up to the final scene, we are led to believe that the photographer is indeed interested only in the money he can make from the story.

In his introductory essay to *The Movie Book of Film Noir*, Michael Walker summarizes the features that earlier critics had identified as characteristic of the genre: motif, tone, iconography, visual style, mood, characterization, social background, cultural influences (the 'hardboiled' tradition), narrative, representation, paranoia . . . In every respect, Melville's film conforms to the classic pattern. Using a simple device to get the two Frenchmen into an American urban setting, it revolves around the activities of those familiar 'heroes' of 1940s *film noir*, the investigative newsmen, involving them in a narrative based on the equally familiar theme of a mysterious disappearance which brings them into contact, successively, with the classic female characters of the genre: the singer, the call-girl, the nightclub dancer and the minor actress — a victim, as usual, since she tries to commit suicide.

An insistent jazz soundtrack establishes the mood. Apart from brief scenes over the opening credits and at the end, all the action takes place at night — here, in contrast to the sunshine of *A bout de souffle*, we have the *noirceur* that properly belongs to *film noir*, with all the expected elements of its 'visual iconography': the Manhattan skyline, the flashing neon lights outside night clubs or on advertisements, the AFP newsroom, the dingy hotel bedrooms, the whisky bottles in sleazy bars, the car headlights and windscreen wipers on rainswept streets, the theatre wings and dressing rooms (contrasted with the light and glamour on stage), the luxurious home where the diplomat's wife is waiting for his return. And we have the 'visual style', with high or low-angle shots, high contrast lighting and the occasional disquieting camera angle of expressionist *film noir*. The main visual clue to the film's date and nationality are a shot of the actress' naked breasts, a hint of lesbianism and a scene in a brothel, all of which would have succumbed to the Hays Code or the British Board of Film Censors. Otherwise (and deprived of its dialogue), this is a Hollywood studio movie.

What of paranoia? One would hardly expect Melville's film to exhibit the anti-communist hysteria of some American 1940s movies. As for its attitude to sexual relationships, while not as sunny as the (essentially) student sex in *A bout de souffle*, it seems uninhibited, with few menacing undertones. The photographer, Delmas (Grasset), shows that he can be rough with women: this is only a pointer to the hardboiled newsman. When we first discover him, he is in bed with a girl and a hangover, and treats both as mildly annoying, but inevitable facts of life: at the time, this attitude would pass as the sign of a balanced male personality.

On closer examination, however, the political themes prove to be more interesting than they may have seemed at first sight. It may be surprising to a modern audience that the moral argument of the film should revolve around the question of whether to publish evidence which is true, but incriminating to a war hero: a magazine in the 1990s has less scruples about printing a good story based on no more than rumour, and would consider itself duty bound to expose one that was verifiable (if only to pre-empt its rivals). Yet, in the end, Delmas throws away his photographs and walks off, laughing (at his own sentimentality?), into the cold light of a Manhattan dawn.

Before that, the action has been held up for the three protagonists to debate the issue. Moreau (Melville) sides with his boss, the head of the AFP bureau, who tells the two newsmen about the dead diplomat's past: a man of the old school, statesman rather than politician, he joined de Gaulle's Free French Forces and went on a mission to occupied France, where he was responsible for persuading the communist Resistance and the right to combine against the common enemy. He was a man of vision and faith in the future of his country, the AFP boss insists; it is wrong that he should be remembered as an adulterer. In a further twist, we later discover that the diplomat's wife is not aware of his affair, but that his daughter did know about it.

Melville had worked with the Resistance. The struggle involved alliances, not only between communists and catholics, or right-wing liberals, but also in some areas with the criminal underworld — Melville heard stories and made contacts that were to prove useful to a director of crime thrillers. But what does this debate signify in 1959, the year after de Gaulle's return to power? Perhaps the film reflects a certain cynicism about the venality of politicians and offers a plea for national unity behind a statesmanlike leader, regardless of his shortcomings (which is not to imply, of course, that Melville or anyone else could suspect de Gaulle of some sexual misdemeanour). Despite having the look and narrative features of 1940s *film noir*, the film centres on a political and ethical issue which is relevant to 1950s France.

It made virtually no impact there, still less abroad; but the arrival of *A bout de souffle* in Britain and the United States, some two years after its release in France, marked an emphatic divide in critical opinion. Reviewers had found it relatively easy to accept some of the finest early works of the New Wave, notably François Truffaut's *Les Quatre cents coups*, Chabrol's *Le Beau Serge* and even Alain Resnais' *Hiroshima mon amour*, despite the novelties of style: Dilys Powell, in *The Sunday Times*, welcomed *Hiroshima* as 'Proustian', 'a savage experience' and 'a complex work', and was equally enthusiastic two years later about Alain Robbe-Grillet's *L'Année dernière à Marienbad* — 'audacious and lovely', comparable to 'an obscure but splendid poem'. But these were films that fitted pre-existing notions of what 'art' films should be about: social problems, childhood alienation, catholic feelings of guilt, stories of love and war, psychological analysis, memory, imagination, eroticism (linked, in the case of Resnais and Robbe-Grillet, to the French New Novel). The style might be disconcerting, but the theoretical and literary antecedents were identifiable and reassuring.

'Perhaps he thinks it a work of art', Ernest Betts scoffed in *The People* (July 9, 1961), questioning the British censor's decision to pass *A bout de souffle*, a film 'entirely without scruples or morals'. It is the cry of a man who, for some years, must have seen his ethical standards challenged by violence and eroticism in 'Continental movies' which were defended by more intellectual critics on the grounds of artistic merit; and it is the sneer of a man who feels, at last, that his ground is sure — with a film that has no 'literary' pretentions, announcing its debt to a minor American studio specializing in the cinema equivalent to the pulp novel.

It was not only the popular press that rounded on Godard; left-wing journals, right-wing journals and even Dilys Powell found fault with *A bout de souffle*, for what, at base, are the same ideological or ethical reasons as those that inspired Betts. In *The Sunday Telegraph* (July 9, 1961), Alan Dent argued that Godard's use of the Mozart clarinet concerto 'shows up the whole 'beatnik' business for the baseness that it is, and may be said to give the film a knock-out blow from which it never recovers.' In the left-wing weekly *Tribune* (June 21, 1961), Boleslaw Sulik defined Godard's ideology as 'right-wing anarchism' — 'a synthetic outlook, made up of digested pulp fiction and American "B" films', which 'touches human experience only in sexual relations and from there trails off into adolescent dreams.' Also from the left, in *The New Statesman*, William Whitebait asked: 'Must we bow down yet again to the fascination of old Hollywood gangster films . . .?'; while *The Times* (July 7, 1961, its critics anonymous in those days), saw it as 'a film in the veins of which runs not the healthy, turbulent blood of anarchy, but the thin, grey fluid of nihilism.' You may wonder how often *The Times* had previously found cause to speak with such approval of 'the healthy, turbulent blood of anarchy'.

From the other side of the fence (and the pond), we have *Time* (February 17, 1961): 'heart-stopping energy and eye-opening originality . . . daringly cubistic'; and Roger Angell in *The New Yorker* (February 11, 1961): 'far and away the most brilliant, most intelligent and most exciting movie I have encountered this season'. The division is not only one between British and American writers, but (quite clearly) between those who see form as more important than content, and vice versa. Angell emphasizes the point in a long analysis of the bedroom scene between Seberg and Belmondo, concluding: 'At the end of this, we have not only understood the murderer and his girl-friend for the self-destructive, attractive and frightening narcissists that they are; we have, to a large degree, *become* them.' It would be hard to conceive a more overt expression of the fear haunting his British colleagues: that the audience for such a film, protected by none of the distancing effects of a respectable literary source or pretentious obscurities, would succumb to the attraction of the hero and heroine's frighteningly destructive narcissism.

Dilys Powell adopts what might be called a 'mid-Atlantic'

stance: 'This is the crest of the New Wave; incalculable, violent, self-expending', which 'looks only at the cold and brutal surface of life . . . The young generation of French film-makers is occupied in a process of disengagement.' She sets *A bout de souffle* in contrast to the 'sentimental cinema of right and wrong', which had its own truth, while this has its own way of telling lies: 'in spite of the undeniable brilliance of form and style, it remains no more than a superb pattern; a pattern of dried leaves cast on the surface of water. There is a closer approach to human truth in the nonsense of *The Singing Fool.*'

The disengagement is not only on the part of French film-makers; we are here at the start of a long process of disengagement by the critics, who over the next three decades were to come under increasing attack for their literary background and bias; find themselves obliged to accept greater and greater levels of violence and eroticism in the cinema; and witness a breakdown in the distinction between high art and popular culture. The certainties of the 1950s, when to describe something as 'pulp fiction' or 'novelettish' was a sound condemnation, are vanishing, together with the 'standards' of a time when film reviewers were still shocked by nudity and violence — or pretended to be shocked — and condemned them with what they assumed was the voice of public opinion. With the decline in cinema audiences, the focus of the debate on 'effects' of screen violence and eroticism had shifted, in any case, towards television.

The ground had been prepared, particularly, by the writers of *Cahiers du cinéma*, with their reappraisal of Hollywood, the *auteur* theory, the insistence that the criteria for judging films were different from those of judging literature. It was underpinned, too, by the theoretical arguments of French structuralism which challenged the established canon of high art. But what is lost is something in the sense of evil that informed the classic *film noir*; and, more than that, a sense of transgression of codes. The villains had once been explicitly destructive and sinful, but their allure, like that of Satan in *Paradise Lost*, was hidden, something too disturbing to be openly acknowledged or understood even by their creators. With *A bout de souffle*, the nihilistic killer portrayed by Belmondo can be openly both attractive and frightening, the destructiveness part of his appeal, just as it is part of his style. And it is on that above all — even exclusively — that he asks to be judged.

To say that is not to concur with the reviewers who condemned Godard's film as base and immoral, but to point up a watershed in attitudes. The divide is clearer in the British press, where it was longer delayed because of a greater conformism and certain pre-conceptions about 'foreign' or 'art' movies. But some of the critical reaction to *A bout de souffle* in France followed similar lines, Gérard Bonnet (in *Les Temps modernes*, April-May, 1960) speaking of 'the priority given to effect, this taste for style', and asking whether we should rejoice at Godard's demonstration that in future 'there will be no other human reality than that which the cinema can express.'

The divide is one that will widen with time, between the films that continue to use the medium as a means to understand the subject-matter of the genre, and those that use it to deconstruct the genre — to explore the medium itself. In no other cinematic or literary genre are moral concerns so clearly central: stories about crime deal specifically with issues of good and evil, justice and illegality. But a work of genre fiction is, by its nature, the product of a structure which exists by reference to other examples in the genre, and this makes it possible (and even attractive) to engage only with the structures. When Louis Malle made *Ascenseur pour l'échafaud*, Georges Sadoul felt that the subject had been imposed on him by his producers, as suitably 'commercial' (*Les Lettres françaises*, January 30, 1958), because he was a young director making his first film: a genre picture, in other words, could be seen as an exercise, a playful exploration of possibilities, rather than a 'serious' piece of work on a serious theme. Yet the references in Malle's film (to American B-movies, to Bresson) are not the story; they merely help to tell it. In Godard, cross-references become the subject-matter of the film.

Six years after *A bout de souffle*, Godard cast Belmondo in a very similar role for *Pierrot le fou* (1965). Now a married man, but feeling trapped by the monotony of bourgeois life, the character (Ferdinand, but renamed Pierrot by his lover, Marianne) goes with his wife to a party where they meet the film director Samuel Fuller, allegedly in Paris to film *Les Fleurs du mal*. 'A film,' Fuller tells him, 'is like a battleground: love, hate, action, violence, death — in a word, emotions.' Bored with the conversation, Ferdinand leaves his wife at the party, flirting with another man, and goes home. There he picks up the babysitter, Marianne Renoir (Anna Karina), his former lover, and offers to drive her home. He spends the night with her and in the morning (like several fictional heroes since Richard Hannay in John Buchan's *The Thirty-Nine Steps*), he discovers a dead body in the apartment and, sprayed on the wall, the letters OAS-IS (a common adjustment of the OAS slogan). With a caseful of money and pursued by a group of gangsters or terrorists, the couple set off for the South of France on a romantic spree, robbing a petrol station, burning the car and the money and settling on an idyllic island off the coast.

The acknowledged source for this story is a thriller by Lionel White, *Obsession*: a middle-class American leaves his wife and flees to Las Vegas with a gangster's moll, who takes advantage of his infatuation to make him the fall-guy in a robbery. In fact, this source has little more significance than any of the other references to books, paintings, music and current affairs scattered through the film: when it opens, Ferdinand/Pierrot is in his bath, reading to his children from a book about Velasquez; Marianne's second name is Renoir; he mentions *Johnny Guitar* and *César Birotteau*; she uses a trick learned from Laurel and Hardy to knock out the petrol station attendant; there are snatches of Vivaldi, edited like pieces of film; Vietnam, the Algerian War, American Imperialism and Godard's other concerns in the mid-1960s litter the screen like jottings in a diary. With his cameraman Raoul Coutard, he has learned to use colour in an imaginative and original way — it is not blood we see in *Pierrot*, he told one interviewer, 'but red'.

'I don't really like telling a story,' Godard also remarked (unnecessarily), and expanded on the reference to Velasquez by saying that, towards the end of his life, the artist 'was no longer painting definite things, but what is to be found between definite things.' Where a conventional thriller would have set out to uncover the reason for the corpse in Marianne's apartment, or made Pierrot demand an explanation from her (which might turn out later to have been true or false), *Pierrot le fou* expects him — and us — to be content with her off-hand remark that it is *'une histoire compliquée,'* and something to do with *le trafic d'armes* — no explanation at all, in fact, but another door momentarily ajar on the shady world of the international arms trade.

What is the significance of this accumulation of obliquely opening and closing doors? When a theologian refers to 'the Thomist interpretation of the doctrine of transubstantiation', or a mathematician to 'binomial theorem', or a literary scholar to 'the pathetic fallacy in Wordworth's *Prelude*', they will expect their audience to have an understanding of these concepts and to build on it to achieve some deeper understanding. In such discourse, which is not only pedagogical, but the discourse of many forms of debate, the argument proceeds like the plot of a narrative, starting from certain assumptions and establishing a set of premises which it subsequently develops towards a conclusion. None of the elements is irrelevant, even those which may be deliberately introduced to mislead or to entertain or to suggest tentative extensions of the argument which are not, for the moment, to be explored.

There is no such argument in Godard. The narrative is 'a kind of tapestry, a background on which I can embroider my own ideas.' The references to cinema, literature, art, politics, music and so on, are not there to mislead, or even to entertain or to suggest depths beyond the surface narrative. Where the theologian, mathematician and scholar (or the pre-modern narrator) operate within a strictly delimited discipline and a shared culture with the audiences they address, Godard's films belong to a culture that has none of these certainties or limitations; in fact, to no delimited 'culture' at all. They address an audience that is used to being subjected to a barrage of information on all subjects and from a variety of sources: radio, film, television, books, photographs, record players, newspapers, paintings, magazines, subtitles, conversations, billboards, advertisements, pamphlets, preachers, gaffiti, letters, memoranda, at home and abroad, in its own language or others. There can be no certainties for the film-maker about the audience — no prior assumptions about what it knows, and no sense in engaging in argument with it. 'Life is its subject,' Godard said of *Pierrot le fou*; so he offers us this life that reflects our fragmented experience. It is irrelevant whether or not we have seen *Johnny Guitar*, read *César Birotteau* or studied Velasquez, and enough, at the most, that we should realize that these are references to some film, some novel, some painter.

Where they derive from and how they got here is a clue less to the film than to its maker(s). When Belmondo, as Pierrot, says '*Allons-y, Alonzo!*', he tells us that this is the sort of Frenchman who will imitate Americanisms like 'See you later, alligator!' (the English subtitle reads: 'Let's go, Joe!'). Yet he is also referring us back to the Belmondo character in *A bout de souffle*, who sets off on his escapade with a '*Maintenant je fonce, Alphonse!*' These glancing reflections, quotations and self-quotations, are not meant to 'delineate' character — which might imply something drawn within an outline — but to colour it. The aim, as Godard says, is life, rather than art; and the Other, in life, is unknowable, at best a construct which we fashion for ourselves from our subjective interpretation of actions, words, gestures, attitudes. Belmondo acting Pierrot, Pierrot acting himself — and (why not?) half-quoting Belmondo in the earlier film — are devices for representing the reality of human character and personality which are, to Godard, closer to the actual way in which we perceive those around us.

This is not to say that Pierrot simply 'is': we perceive him in relation to others, in particular to Marianne. As the film proceeds, and from the conversations between them, we observe that, where she feels for the concrete realities of life (trees, animals and so on), he is more concerned with abstractions. These differences may be either the main cause, or a contributing factor, in the gulf that begins to open between them, just as they may equally be given as reasons why they love one another. There is no easy explanation for any of the emotions they feel, and certainly nothing as simple as the conflict in the original novel between infatuation and betrayal.

Moreover, since Marianne is played by Anna Karina who was Godard's wife from 1961 to 1967, it is easy to detect that there may be an autobiographical element in the story — a possibility that none of Godard's statements about it would deny. If, inevitably, Godard must see the personality of Marianne through his understanding of the personality of Karina, then his depiction of Pierrot is likely to reflect this perception, making Pierrot partly a self-portrait. Is this a more or less coded version of the Godard-Karina relationship, as has been suggested? Instead of being defined, the characters of Belmondo-Pierrot-Godard and Karina-Marianne-Karina disappear down a series of self-reflecting mirrors which suggest the fundamental uncertainty of what we mean by 'character' and the falsity of trying to circumscribe it.

What is most clearly missing in both the characters played by Belmondo, is motive, a crucial element in the delineation of character in conventional narrative. Where the latter reaches for a particular truth about human actions and relationships by simplifying motivation and psychology, Godard's films suggest the complexity and unknowability of what lies behind action. Only one thing is certain about Belmondo-Pierrot-Godard: he wants to be free. Imprisoned in a bourgeois marriage — and a bourgeois film — he breaks away, suddenly, impulsively, with a woman who tells him that she will follow him wherever he goes. He takes with him the baggage of contemporary culture and proceeds to scatter it around the countryside. As we watch, instead of being cheered or flattered by the film's references to our own cultural baggage, we are aware that it is being tossed aside unused. Velasquez? Is he just there because Godard believes that he ended by painting 'what is to be found between definite things'? And were we expected to know that, anyway?

Postmodernism — Godard is somewhere at the point where the concept was starting to be defined — implies a degree of contempt for whatever nostalgia we may feel for the certainties of the past, suggesting that these were always illusions, which have now become impossible to sustain. The life of Godard's characters, like the life of the artist, is a game, which they play knowingly, but to the ultimate. Thus, they are also existential heroes, condemned to freedom. And Godard, like an existentialist himself, was to escape from the dilemma of freedom by becoming increasingly *engagé* as the decade went on, committed to left-wing causes, though not abandoning his playful approach to contemporary culture — merely redefining it as a committed stance towards the bourgeois culture of the West. But for his audience, instead of becoming more meaningful, the films became more tedious as they proclaimed their liberation from narrative, emotion and character. Often stunningly beautiful images are interspersed with wordy passages of debate and disparate fragments from the iconography of contemporary life, leaving no space for reflection on the problems that were once the actual matter of the movies the director admires so much.

François Truffaut's second feature, *Tirez sur le pianiste* (1960), is the other New Wave film (with *A bout de souffle*) that most blatantly acknowledges the influence of the American B-movie. It was adapted from *Down there* by the writer David Goodis; Truffaut had also read Goodis's *Fire in the Flesh* at around this time and made sure that the author was credited on the film poster. But the film moves a long way from the novel, not least in transposing the action to France and including a host of passing references to gangster films, silent cinema, the Marx Brothers, film censorship, Hitchcock and so on. Before shooting started on August 16, 1959, Truffaut said in a letter to the film's star, the singer Charles Aznavour, that he was about to undertake a re-write of the script, adding 'it will be a documentary on timidity'. The central character is, indeed, shy, but the 'timidity' was also the director's. The resulting compound of melodrama, pastiche and ironic, sentimental love story, is also entirely Truffaut's.

His other two clear tributes to American *film noir* were adaptations from Cornell Woolrich (William Irish), *La Mariée était en noir* (1967) and *La Sirène du Mississippi* (1969). Woolrich/Irish was one of the most frequently used writers of pulp fiction in Hollywood during the 1940s, the creator of intricate, ironical stories, the very titles of which often include the words 'black' or 'darkness'. Truffaut transfers the stories to French settings (with the rather obvious contrivance of a boat, called 'La Sirène du Mississippi', to get round the change of location in the second), and lards them with the usual battery of references: to Hitchcock, particularly. The actors (Jeanne Moreau, Claude Rich and Jean-Claude Brialy in the first, Belmondo and Catherine Deneuve in the second) bring their own additional meanings to the films. The theme of the *femme fatale* was one to which Truffaut had given his own significance since *Jules et Jim*, and the music (by Bernard Herrmann and Antoine Duhamel) has become native to France, as much as to anywhere else. By this time, in the 1960s, the American jazz that had sounded so raw and so exotic even in the previous decade — when it evoked the Black nightclubs of Harlem or the neon-lit streets of Manhattan, and when a trumpet playing in the night could conjure up a whole world of sleazy hotel rooms and lonely men or forsaken women; and the big band sound that spoke of American brashness and expensive glamour, or the arrival of overnight trains in Grand Central Station; and the honky-tonk piano; and the blues singer — had all been naturalized, their rough edges smoothed out, and the whole transformed into the international language of dance music and pop.

The absence of music and the use instead of natural sound, are what make Jacques Becker's last film, *Le Trou* (1959), seem at once old-fashioned and 'classical' — his 'most concrete' film, according to Sadoul, 'profound', 'noble', 'virile'; Melville in *Cahiers du cinéma* no. 107 for May 1960, even described it as 'a masterpiece . . . the greatest French film of all time'. There was an obvious debt to Bresson's *Un condamné à mort s'est échappé* (1956): Becker abandoned the earlier film's wartime setting, but added a characteristic theme from the wartime escape movie: that of betrayal. Taken from a true story by José Giovanni (and including one amateur actor, Jean Kéraudy, who took part in the events), it describes the arrival of a new prisoner at the Paris prison of La Santé in 1947. The existing inhabitants of the cell are suspicious of the new man, Gaspard (Marc Michel). All are on remand, though, unlike the rest, Gaspard is not a professional criminal, but a car salesman who is accused of attempting to murder his wife with the complicity of his sister-in-law, who is also his mistress. Manu (Philippe Leroy) is the unacknowledged leader of the group and particularly unwilling to welcome Gaspard. The reason for their mistrust is that they have found an escape route which will eventually take them to freedom, via the 'hole'.

Becker is concerned solely with the interaction of the men and their contrasting personalities. From the very start, in the Governor's office, we see that Gaspard is apologetic and deferential towards authority. He wants to be loved by everybody — authorities and fellow-prisoners — signalling a moral weakness that amounts, in reality, to an inability to feel for anyone except himself. His cellmates cannot go ahead with their escape without him knowing and, when they warn him that he is liable to land a ten-year sentence for his crime, he eagerly agrees to take part. The difference between Gaspard and the others lies in their solidarity with one another — confirmed by the distance they establish between themselves and the warders — and in their skills — demonstrated during a prolonged sequence (as they test the escape route) which recalls both Bresson and *Du rififi chez les hommes*. The absence of background music suggests Dassin, that — and the use of amateur actors — Bresson. When the Governor tells Gaspard that his wife is prepared not to press the charge against him, he is faced with a dilemma, his own interests now being in conflict with those of his cellmates.

Favourable critics spoke of 'austerity', 'sobriety', *'rigueur'* and *'efficacité'*, though the film was not a box-office success on its release. The POW escape movie was always a less popular genre in France than in Britain or America, and by 1960 the appeal of the genre was fading even in those countries. Becker was an 'Old Wave' director who, despite being admired by the critics of *Cahiers du cinéma*, did not share their New Wave romanticism. During the next twenty years, after the death of Becker and Melville, only Bresson would continue to work in the 'classical' tradition, appearing, as a result, increasingly an outsider.

IV.

CRIMINAL TYPES

'After the failure of *Deux hommes dans Manhattan*,' Melville told Claude Beylie in an interview for *L'Avant-scène du cinéma* in 1963, 'I decided only to undertake films intended for a mass audience, and not purely for a small number of enlightened film buffs.' The result was *Le Doulos* (1962).

As the credit sequence tells us, the title means 'the informer' (nark, finger, stool pigeon). Twenty years later, Bob Swaim's *La Balance* (1982) was to take its title from another slang term for the same character, perhaps in tribute to Melville. But some similarity in the two films is probably inevitable. Like the double agent, the police informer belongs to two opposing sides, and his or her world is one of duplicity and betrayal.

The interest of Melville's underworld, like that of Becker, is that it involves the audience in a struggle between good and evil where these do not correspond to legal definitions of right and wrong. The criminals of *Le Doulos*, like those of *Touchez pas au grisbi*, have a code of morality, and it is this rather than the judicial code that provides the ethical criterion against which they are judged. However, while the criminals in *Touchez pas au grisbi* are not bothered by the police, the existence of an informer in *Le Doulos* means that they must be brought directly into the story. This obtrusive presence of the Law means juxtaposing the conventional code with the criminals' own concepts of right, to give a more complex ethical scale: good (crooks), bad (police), evil (informers); with a kind of 'honest' complicity between the honourable soldiers on each side (crooks and police), and a 'dishonest' complicity between the police and their narks. Maurice (Serge Reggiani), who belongs to the first group, actually makes the distinction in the course of the film, telling Inspector Clain (Jean Desailly) that there are *des truands propres* ('clean crooks') and *des salauds*.

Maurice's conversation with Clain displays the mentality of the *truand propre* ('it's a fair cop') to perfection. The two men respect one another as soldiers on opposite sides in a war; our sympathies are weighted towards the criminals because they seem to play fairer, given the context of the struggle, and have a code based on comradeship. We sympathize, too, with their ambitions: like Max in *Grisbi*, Silien (Jean-Paul Belmondo) has a modest ambition — to retire with his girlfriend: 'I've set up a nice house for myself in Ponthierry, by itself, on the hill. I think I'm going to pack it in. In this job you always end up a tramp . . . or with a bullet in you.' However, we suspect that Silien's money (unlike Max's) may not be clean.

The idea that experienced police detectives and professional criminals understand and respect one another had by this time become something of a commonplace. A continuation of war by other means, the conflict between them lifts its participants onto a different plane from the civilians, *les caves*, who watch from the sidelines or the auditorium. *Le Doulos* is a wordy film, combining a number of elements from its predecessors in cinema and literature, among which are this exploration of an understanding across the boundaries of the law: 'he makes us feel, in a way that hardly anyone has done previously, the complicity and comradeship that really exists between criminals and the police,' Robert Chazal commented in *France-Soir* (February 9, 1963). There are also extensive passages of detection, in which the police explain the evidence that leads them to their conclusions — passages of dialogue that sound almost like the revelation scene in a 'country-house' detective novel. And the same explanatory style is used by Silien, to counter the charge that he is an informer. Ingeniously, Melville shows us which side we are on, tricks us into believing that we have a clear case against the central character, then allows him to argue us into an uncertainty that obliges us to choose between mutually exclusive versions of the 'truth'.

'The 'crime', or more precisely the assumed 'crime' with which we are dealing here, is a moral one,' Jean de Baroncelli commented in *Le Monde* (February 14, 1963) — 'moral', both in the sense of 'ethical' and that of 'non-material'. The stool pigeon commits no crime; on the contrary, he upholds the law and tells the truth, but we see him as a cowardly and contemptible figure because his morality is neither the social morality represented by the authorities, nor the individual morality of the underworld. As the participant who most clearly reveals the conflict between the two moral codes — and the ambivalence of our response — the informer could be a central character in the classic *film noir*, but rarely appears as such. There, 'he' is more often 'she': it is the women who are the betrayers in the American model of the genre, and sex is the weakness that allows Delilah to deliver the otherwise invincible Samson to the Philistines.

Silien, whose last thought is for a woman, Fabienne, is a tragic hero like the Gabin of *Le Jour se lève* — or, perhaps, of *La Bête humaine*, depending on whether or not one believes his story. Is he an innocent destroyed by fate, or a traitor who has to suffer for his treachery? Critics at the time were divided on this, and over the merits of Melville's film — either 'classical' or 'mechanical' in its perfection ('Melville forgets the main thing, which is that cinema is not only a craft,' Bernard Dort wrote in the *France-Observateur* for February 14, 1963). The most interesting and significant response came from the left-wing press: Melville demonstrates the narrowness of the gap between the criminals and the police, Henry Chapier wrote in *Combat* (February, 1963) — repeating this not particularly original observation, but adding that the audience was thus led to view wrongdoers, stool pigeons and police with the same mistrust, 'and hence perceive how fragile is the bourgeois morality that salves its conscience when it abominates the "underworld".' An alternative society implies an alternative morality, and (to the extent that they depicted the *Milieu* as a social *milieu*, governed by its own rules of conduct), films like *Le Doulos* anticipated the political messages of post-1968 cinema.

The reaction of Patrick Bureau in the communist weekly *Les Lettres françaises* (February 14, 1963) was hostile. This was not the first time, he said, that Meville had depicted only 'bad heroes': 'gradually, since *Bob le Flambeur* and *Deux hommes dans Manhattan* . . ., down to *Le Doulos*, he has been indulging in a rather disturbing apology for informers' and showing 'rather too much leniency' towards them: 'the ending of *Le Doulos* . . . is a provocation'. The very ambiguity of Melville's story meant that one could choose one's own meaning, and this meaning would shift according to circumstances and points of view.

In our time, Satan descends from the clouds in a silver airplane. Milton's century has nothing to teach our own about his allure, which finds its most perfect expression in the blackest of black films, Leni Riefenstahl's *Triumph of the Will*. What would Satan be if he were not widely mistaken for a god? He manifests himself here in the midst of adoring faces, uplifted arms, marching soldiers, torchlight processions. Many who saw the film when it was released in 1935 shared in this adoration. A few admired its extraordinary technical and artistic qualities. Only after a decade could audiences generally start to appreciate its significance and begin to come to terms with a wickedness that altered for ever our understanding of the human capacity for inhumanity. Our admiration of the film's aesthetic qualities, and the complete reversal of the way in which we perceive the awful beauty of its images, gave new urgency to the question posed by any depiction of evil in art — in appearance, the same question that Shelley had asked about the Satan of *Paradise Lost*.

However, the revelation of the horror of the extermination camps posed a different, and far more challenging question. It was not too hard to come to terms with the allure of power; but the problem was not the charisma of the Prince of Darkness, so much as the inadequacy of Adolf Hitler to fill the role and the capacity for evil shown by his minions. Even before his defeat, notably in Chaplin's *The Great Dictator*, and with added mystery afterwards when the extent of his crimes was revealed, Hitler looked on the surface like a figure of fun: the Chaplinesque moustache, the dainty cough, the tedious table talk, the liking for cream cakes, the probable sexual inadequacies, the neat watercolours, the Munich dosshouse, the taste for kitsch in music and art, the vastly inflated sense of grandeur and self-importance — all these belonged to the personality of a man who might just have risen to become a Bavarian burgomaster or an Austrian shopkeeper, lower middle-class, pretentious, prim, conventional, with a tendency to strut and deliver himself of his opinionated views to a few sympathetic friends in the *Bierkeller*. Looking at *Triumph of the Will* after the event, we strain to perceive a figure of immense and evil power. The power lies in the vast masses that he was able to mobilize, and the mystery is how he managed to do it.

Behind him were those ranks of equally unimposing men, Goebbels the minor intellectual, Eichmann the bureaucrat, Himmler the chicken farmer, and the rest, who worried about the details of rail transportation, supplies of gas, the design of lorries, the efficiency of incinerators, the mechanics and technicalities of their job, its complex economics, while never seemingly concerned with the simple ethics of mass murder. Were human beings — so ordinary that they resembled our next-door neighbours and ourselves — capable of such monstrous inhumanity? The Satanic bureaucrat, the Satanic stationmaster: the phrase, 'the banality of evil', has become a cliché; the very notion is banal.

This was a new lesson, after the well-known one about the fascination of evil, which the triumph of Hitler's will had merely confirmed. Not that it had previously been necessary for every fictional criminal to be Moriarty or Dr Fu Manchu: the bad guys in gangster movies were often just thugs, the killers in Simenon's novels usually little men. There were also the real-life cases of murderers like Crippen and Landru (the second of these portrayed in Chaplin's 1947 film, *Monsieur Verdoux* and in Chabrol's *Landru* of 1962); and the war gave an incidental opportunity to Dr Petiot, a French multiple-murderer who killed Jews during the Occupation, after pretending that he could help them escape. Anyone could have had Dr Petiot for a neighbour.

This is not the point, however. The Moriartys and Fu Manchus were personifications of evil, with a grandeur that meant their deeds needed no explanation: they belonged to a time and a genre (melodrama) that took for granted the existence of the force that they represented, underpinned by the ideology of religion. The behaviour of less imposing criminals needed some justification and here rationality was able to supply it: the actions of gangsters could be explained by their social background, those of other killers by some form of clinical madness, or the overpowering influence of everyday motives like sex and greed.

In any case, the creators of fictional worlds prefer them to contain comprehensible explanations for the events that take place in them; hence the tendency of the thriller genres to lean towards particular scientific disciplines: the gangster movie towards politics and sociology, the 'psychological' thriller towards psychoanalysis and the pathology of madness, the (country house) detective thriller towards mathematical logic. The actions of the killer in *Psycho* are not really 'explained' by his fixation on his mother, any more than those of *La Bête humaine* are 'explained' by tainted heredity, those of the murderer in *La Nuit du carrefour* by greed and drugs, or those of the gangster in Claude Sautet's *Classe tous risques* (1959) by social alienation; but these tentative 'explanations' ensure that the audience is not left without the reassurance of some coherence in the fictional world. At times, the tendency may be accentuated, the gangster movie become more clearly a political allegory, the psychological thriller a study in psychopathology, the mystery story a mere intellectual puzzle in which the motives of desire for money or sex are simply givens; or, by reaction, the drift may be reversed and the motives explored within one sub-genre by reference to the conventions of another.

What is disorienting, however, is the story that refuses to explain, or provides explanations that are contradictory and inadequate. This is the 'amorality' that critics perceived in *A bout de souffle* — in the film itself, not the character played by Belmondo. The killing of the policeman would have been easy for Godard to explain, had he wished: panic, sadism, madness, an unhappy childhood, a criminal teenage subculture, any of which would then have been carried through into the remainder of the film, constructing a consistent profile for the character. Instead, Godard observes the commission of a gratuitous act of violence, builds a love story around it and allows his 'hero' a sort of innocence that belies what he has done. The nearest we get to an explanation is that he sees himself as a character in an American gangster movie; and, in a work that is so patently a homage to the genre, this hardly amounts to a message with reassuring implications.

Belmondo is one of the three major international male film

stars that France has produced, all three tending at some point in their careers to be typecast as criminal outsiders and *marginaux*, and all three managing to achieve international success largely without succumbing to the temptation of Hollywood. The first, of course, was Gabin, the 'innocent' outlaw of *Pépé-le-Moko*, *Le Jour se lève* and even *La Bête humaine* (where, in what was to become a fixed element in the character, he is 'innocented' by love); he later matured into the older criminal of *Touchez pas au grisbi* and the Godfather of *Le Clan des siciliens*. The New Wave version was Belmondo, his post-New Wave successor, Gérard Depardieu.

At the start of his career, Depardieu appeared in films with both Gabin and Belmondo, usually cast as a hoodlum. He was physically suited to the type, and in fact got his first film rôle in 1965 because director Roger Leenhardt wanted someone to play the beatnik in his short *Le Beatnik et le minet*, and Depardieu had the right qualifications. The son of an illiterate metalworker from Châteauroux, he had himself had a few minor brushes with the law in the course of a disorderly adolescence, not overloaded with schoolwork. In a country where actors usually suggested at least a degree of intellectuality and sophistication, Depardieu came across as boorish, sensual, disrespectful of authority and tradition, heavy in physique, but capable at moments of surprising delicacy of gesture and of feeling — in short, rather un-French, but interesting and perhaps representative of a new working class that had grown up under de Gaulle and matured during the 'events' of 1968.

Just as Belmondo had been a less scrupulous version of the character played by the young Gabin, so Depardieu became a less polished version of Belmondo, distinct from his two predecessors particularly in his attitude towards women. His cinema debut coincided with a relaxation in censorship, and in the period between that and the consolidation of the feminist movement, his machismo could be explicitly displayed. Sexual freedom was an essential element in the anti-authoritarianism of the generation of '68, whose heroes came in two shapes: the overtly political and the instinctively political. Depardieu was easily typecast as an instinctive anarchist.

After small parts in films like *Le Tueur* (1972) and *Les Gaspards* (1974), and a less predictable rôle in Marguerite Duras' *Nathalie Granger* (1973) which showed him to have a wider range than one might have expected, he achieved his first major success with Bertrand Blier's *Les Valseuses* (1974), playing opposite his friends Patrick Dewaere and Miou-Miou (with Jeanne Moreau, as an ex-jailbird, appearing like a refugee from thrillers past). The two men messed around on set like rebellious adolescents, at times seeming unable to distinguish between real-life and the characters they were playing. After Dewaere's suicide eight years later, Depardieu wrote an open letter to him, suggesting that his friend had died because of an inability to cope with this confusion between fiction and life.

Dewaere and Depardieu play two young hooligans who have an utter contempt for the conventions of French bourgeois life: 'no mistaking it — this is France!' one of them exclaims after one manifestation of repectability. They steal a car, go joy-riding in it, then return it to its owner, who responds with typically bourgeois humourlessness by drawing a gun on them and threatening to hand them over to the police. They manage to turn the tables on him and run off with his girlfriend (Miou-Miou) — the assumption, throughout the film, being that any woman would be grateful for the opportunity to sleep with Depardieu or Dewaere. But Dewaere has been shot in the groin (*'les valseuses'* means 'testicles', as well as 'waltzers', the title combining the film's two motifs: sex and the merry romp that the young men take through the French countryside); he is afraid that his virility may have been impaired. Eventually, he has the opportunity to dispel his fears.

Despite the relaxation in censorship in the preceding decade, the film's bad language and explicit sex were shocking when it was released; but this is not especially important in the present context. *Les Valseuses* is a film which involves crime and criminals only in a technical sense: the viewpoint of the *marginal*, which the film openly adopts, takes the ambivalence over wrongdoing latent in many earlier crime films, and develops it, effectively criminalizing society itself for its repression of the life-affirming qualities of freedom and honesty: as the story develops, we realize that Depardieu and Dewaere, in spite of their coarseness, are not simply *je m'en foutistes* like Belmondo in *A bout de souffle* or *Pierrot le fou*; they are caring, sensitive and, according to their lights, moral in a way that the bourgeois whom they encounter are not. And, with this, the (however tenuous) hold that the crime film or thriller had retained on distinctions of right and wrong, legality and illegality, is lost, and we enter a political realm where the underlying concern is to explore the mentality of a 'criminal society', rather than the mentality of the criminal, as previously understood. The leading characters in *Les Valseuses* are criminal only because a stifling regime gives them no alternative except to rebel or to sacrifice all freedom and integrity.

In Alfred Hitchcock's film *Shadow of a Doubt* (1943), the seductive but mysterious Uncle Charlie (Joseph Cotten) comes back to the small town where his married sister lives with her husband and children, the elder of whom is a teenage daughter, also called 'Charlie'. Young Charlie hates the stifling atmosphere of Middle America: her dull father and the friends whom he meets after work for discussions about gruesome crimes; her mother, no less stifled and frustrated, but resigned to the fate that awaits Charlie herself if she cannot escape. Uncle Charlie, her namesake, is a breath of fresh air.

What Charlie does not know is that her Uncle Charlie's charm is that of a psycopath. He arrives in town followed by the young policeman (Macdonald Carey) investigating a series of 'Merry Widow' killings. Many of Hitchcock's favourite themes are here: the explicit identification of the two Charlies (innocent young girl, insane older man), the façade of bourgeois life, the black humour, the unknowability of the 'other' — and the suspense created by the potential young victim's trust as it gives way to suspicion: can Uncle Charlie afford to let her live, once she has the evidence that will make her suspicions certainties? Will the handsome young cop, with whom she is falling in love, be in time to save her?

François Truffaut admired Hitchcock and published his interviews with him, but the Frenchman who has used Hitchcock most is Claude Chabrol (who also in 1957 wrote a book on the English director, in collaboration with Eric Rohmer). The idea of transfer of guilt was evident in his first feature, *Le Beau Serge* (1958), and he returned to the provinces for a film that is so close to *Shadow of a Doubt* in its dominant motifs as to be almost a remake: *Le Boucher* (1969); almost, but not quite.

Stéphane Audran plays Hélène, a primary school teacher in a community whose daily life is meticulously observed. This is both literally Sarlat and metaphorically the whole of provincial France: the quiet town square, enclosed in its eighteenth-century buildings, the chickens feeding in the fields, the bells of school and church, and the chiming clocks, measuring out the lives of the children in the playground, all adding up to a world of solidity and rationality in harmony with Hélène's work as she asks her class to take a dictation from Balzac (though, on closer examination, the text itself, and the fact that the woman in it is also named 'Hélène', are not entirely reassuring; nor is the discordant music that breaks out at intervals through the film; and, on second thoughts, the bells). The story begins with the marriage of Hélène's male colleague, Léon, a country wedding that, in these surroundings, seems to promise the couple a future of tranquil contentment.

The Uncle Charlie in this agreeable setting is Paul (Jean Yanne), the butcher who has recently returned after serving with the Army in the colonial wars in Indochina and Algeria. 'Popaul', we gradually realize, is neither rational nor harmonious: he was employed during the wars not as a soldier, but as a butcher, yet he talks of the terrible atrocities he has seen done to women and children. He claims to admire 'two things that one doesn't have in the Army: logic and freedom'; but he served for fifteen years, (though hating it) because 'I was stupid'. His mystery, more than that, is inherent in his trade — what could be better, Hélène asks, than to have your meat chosen for you by a butcher; and he brings her a leg of lamb, which he gives her in front of her class of eleven or twelve-year olds — a symbolic gesture that reminds us of the daily violence that has to be inflicted for the sake of our stomachs; and we shall have further reminders that the civilization represented by the tranquil life of the town is no more than a façade.

The first murder of a young woman is attributed to a tramp, and naturally becomes the subject of local gossip: like Hitchcock, Chabrol mirrors his audience in the supporting characters, for whom murder stories hold a morbid fascination. Popaul has started to attach himself to Hélène, accompanying her on outings with the children, cooking for her with professional expertise. The school prepares for a fancy-dress pageant and, as the participants dance a minuet, the music for just this one moment is allowed to suggest order and harmony. It is a brief respite, however, because the scene is followed by a school visit to see prehistoric cave paintings and the discovery by the children of a second body (in a Grand Guignolesque incident of dripping blood); the victim is Léon's young wife.

Hélène's suspicions about Popaul are aroused, allayed and finally confirmed; but, unlike Young Charlie, she is given no convenient means of escape into the arms of a handsome policeman. Chabrol employs some well-tried devices to associate the audience with her uncertainty and her fear, but without developing her character enough for us to identify with her at any deeper level: her feelings remain impenetrable and she serves primarily as a standpoint from which we can study Popaul. Is she in love with him, or is she afraid of love, as she implies in their one intimate conversation, when she says that after a disappointment many years before she has wanted to avoid being hurt? 'I loved her so much,' Léon tells Hélène at his wife's funeral, in what sounds like a formal expression of grief rather than the outpouring of uncontrollable passion. The constraints of civilization do not make life itself less savage, they can only draw a veil over our appetites. 'You must realize,' Hélène tells her pupils, 'that the instincts, feelings and even the intellect of Cro-Magnon man were entirely human; the only difference is to do with subsistence.' And, conversely, we — as humans — remain meat-eating savages, despite our greater delicacy in dealing with the fact — 'I'm sure he was very nice,' one of Hélène's pupils says of primitive man, just as she is about to be shown evidence of the savagery of his modern counterpart. The fundamental dilemma does not go away: it is, as Popaul tells Hélène, that 'not making love drives you nuts', while she replies, 'making love can also drive you crazy'.

It seemed worthwhile to state explicitly what one means by describing Chabrol's film as 'Hitchcockian': the comparison with *Shadow of a Doubt* shows how much *Le Boucher* owes to it, while at the same time revealing the essential differences between them. The premise of the two films is the same: small town, innocent female character, arrival of mysterious male outsider who becomes the focus of the female's attention while at the same time arousing suspicion in her and creating suspense for the audience. But where Hitchcock resolves the mystery in a conventional happy ending, Chabrol rejects this form of closure, because he is concerned not only with the unknowability of the 'other', but with exploring the widest implications suggested by the theme of transfer of guilt: the actions of the criminal, like those of the Nazi concentration camp guards, reflect on the nature of us all: *homo sum, et nihil humanum mihi alienum puto.*

Uncle Charlie is a puzzle rather than a mystery; his

dominant characteristic is narcissistic greed, rather than lust. The puzzle is his ability to charm others and engage with them, while remaining himself unengaged: the centre is utterly cold and detached. Popaul's ancestor, at a more profound level, is Lantier from *La Bête humaine*: both men have the 'instincts and feelings' of Cro-Magnon man and are redeemed by their love for a woman which, in the last resort, drives them to sacrifice themselves in order to save her from impulses that they cannot control. We learn to hate and fear Uncle Charlie, but our sympathy never deserts Lantier or Popaul.

Zola, however, provided an explanation for Lantier, in his 'tainted' heredity, that closes off the narrative of *La Bête humaine*. Chabrol produces similar explanations for Popaul, then carefully discards them. The most obvious is the 'liberal' thesis: Popaul has seen terrible atrocities in Indo-china and Algeria, so perhaps he has been corrupted by the colonial system. But this will simply not do: he makes clear that he was not a combat soldier but employed by the Army in his civilian job; and, in any case, if some soldiers are corrupted by killing, then why some and not all? There is no neat explanation, from cause and effect, for this likeable man who goes to his death saying that all blood, whether animal or human, has the same smell.

The police and the townspeople do not even see the killer as a puzzle: he is simply *le sadique*, a vicious murderer. In the end, this is how Hitchcock allows us to perceive Uncle Charlie — as the 'beast' of newspaper headlines; but not, in the case of Popaul, Chabrol. The open ending of *Le Boucher* leaves us with a mystery unsolved: 'Ah, Mademoiselle, if you only knew what we see, what we rub shoulders with, if you only knew what human nature is capable of . . .', the inspector tells Hélène, when she rejects his suggestion that Léon might be the killer. The only thing that puzzles him is that the victims have not been raped; and it puzzles us, because it removes yet another possible explanation for Popaul's behaviour. We are left, instead, with the impenetrable mystery of a man who is capable of the greatest wickedness (sacrificing others to his needs) and the greatest altruism (sacrificing himself to love); who is stifled by the need for blood, yet fainted at the sight of it when he was a child; who refuses to make the conventional distinction between the killing of a young woman and the killing of a lamb.

Civilized life demands that we should be like Hélène, who cries at the slaughter of her colleague's wife, yet is cheered up when Popaul tells her that he has seen some lambs in Périgueux that would make a nice *gigot*. Of course she is right: we need to identify with our own species and to ignore the fact that all blood has the same smell, so as to maintain some semblance of order in a chaotic universe. Yet we find the sensible middle way at the expense of honesty and passion, as well as wickedness: Popaul suggests an answer, of a kind, to some premises of *film noir*: the ambivalence of our perception of evil, the savagery that lurks (in perhaps more concentrated form) at the heart of urban or 'civilized' living.

What we remember, best of all, are the rich colours of Sarlat and the picture postcard beauty of the town, counterpointed by the disturbing emptiness of its streets and the discordant music that punctuates the film; and counterpointed too by the cold, night-time colours of the ending, the modern hospital building, the final view across the river at dawn, with the word '*fin*' neatly inscribed in one corner. This is not an ending, but a philosophical question, expressed in abstract, almost mathematical terms. Cro-Magnon man, Hélène has told her pupils, was saved by 'his aspirations' for a better future, without which we would not exist. How bright are those aspirations now; and, without them, what is left for us?

'Nothing more than a straightforward and highly enjoyable thriller,' was *The Spectator*'s verdict on *Le Boucher* (June 7, 1972), while John Coleman, in *The New Statesman* (June 16,

1972) found 'the psychological underpinnings both sketchy and shaky' — a common reaction to Chabrol's refusal of the closure that would have been provided by a coherent explanation for Popaul's crimes and a more positive response from Hélène. *Le Figaro*, on the other hand, had described it as the best French film since the Liberation, and it was highly praised, from the other end of the political spectrum, by *Les Lettres françaises* (March 3, 1970) which spoke of 'impeccable craftsmanship, taking us . . . from a simple love story to a bloodstained tragedy.' Chabrol had fallen out of favour, however, with *Cahiers du cinéma*.

The age was more overtly political, and critics tended to look to underlying social causes rather than individual psychology or motivation. The 1970s were to be the period of the police procedural (though often without the approval of police methods that is usually an assumption of that genre, making what might be called — in more senses than one — an 'anti-police' procedural); or that of the anarchist anti-hero, a development from the characters outlined in *A bout de souffle* and *Les Valseuses*. This was the period, too, of the overtly political thriller, exemplified by Costa-Gavras' *Z* (1968), and the gangster movie in which one could read covert political implications. Alain Delon — who in real life as a teenager had allegedly frequented the Marseille *milieu* and who was involved in a scandal with alleged underworld connections in 1968 when his bodyguard was found murdered — became typecast as the cold killer, *Le Samouraï*, though he was equally capable of playing the cop in Melville's *Un flic* (1972), embittered and embroiled with a drug baron's mistress (Catherine Deneuve). There had never been an absolutely clear line between the two sides of the law, but it was now still further erased.

These tendencies might be as much in the way that films were read as in the way they were made. Directors continued to work in traditional forms and according to established formulae, for much the same reason that they had always exploited the conventions of Hollywood thrillers, *films noirs* and other genres: the cinema audience demanded particular types of entertainment and, like all art forms, cinema is partly self-referential, speaking a language that derives its meanings from what has gone before, not from 'real life'. Even a French audience would understand the situations in *Le Boucher* (small town, provincial school-teacher, murders, evidence, suspect, woman in danger and so on) more through its knowledge of Hitchcock's American thrillers or other French works in the genre, than from personal experience. The 1960s also saw revivals of a figure from the days of French silent cinema: Georges Franju's *Judex* (1963), based on the *cinéromans* of Louis Feuillade (1917) and coming at a time when popular literature generally, and strip cartoons in particular, were starting to be taken more seriously in France. An example is Alain Jessua's *Jeu de massacre* (1967), in which a strip artist's imaginary world starts to invade his life. Jessua's inventive film acknowledged a literary/artistic form in which France excelled and Franju's remake implied the recognition of a specifically national tradition in the cinema thriller.

Revivals and continuations of established forms were ways of tackling the old questions: as Franju himself remarked, referring to *Judex* (in *Cahiers du cinéma*, November 1963), the lawmakers in such films, though they might triumph at the end, were static characters, while the criminal, whose destiny was to be punished, was for the period of the story dynamic and superior: 'in any case, we might as well admit that the incarnation of evil is more attractive than the incarnation of good.'

So it was perfectly possible to go on worrying at the old problem — why do we find evil more seductive than good? — though it was increasingly less possible to do so except within frameworks that were clearly formulaic (the old goodies-and-baddies, cops-and-robbers movies) or, as in the case of *Judex*, with a knowing wink: while Feuillade's *Judex* was a thriller, Franju's is a self-conscious 'thriller', deliberately exploiting our knowledge of the earlier version — just as what was perceived as tragedy by a nineteenth-century audience may now be played (can now only be played) as melodrama; in other words, inevitably adding an element of camp. To be wholly serious, one had to tackle the more fundamental problem: what is the nature of 'good' and 'evil'? And to discover, as Chabrol did in *Le Boucher*, that our own nature makes us all guilty, so that good and evil can coexist bewilderingly in a single person; or to imply that 'good' and 'evil' relate to actions, not personalities, and are the function of a genre, defined by the rôles that we are allocated (Belmondo, the rôle-playing 'baddie' in *A bout de souffle*); and, hence, that these definitions are not moral so much as sociological and political.

Changing the questions meant changing other givens as well. In the American *film noir* of the 1940s, the urban setting was a site of wickedness, inhabited by gangsters, prowlers, killers, the dispossessed, the rootless. The urban private eye, though on the right side of the law, was perilously close to those on the wrong side and the criminal was quite often an ex-cop. In Becker's *Casque d'or*, the small town is an idyllic refuge from the criminal underworld of Paris, but there was also a well-established contrary tradition in France, that of the provincial poison pen (*Le Corbeau*) and the murderous peasant (*Goupi Mains Rouges*); as in England, where the tranquil village was a routine setting for murder. Hitchcock — who, being British, lacked any romantic preconceptions about the virtues of American small town life — imported this European perception of what may lurk beneath the surface of provincial respectability. It was a productive discovery (as we have seen recently in David Lynch's *Twin Peaks*), which fed into *Le Boucher*.

The French mental map during the period from the Revolution to the Fifth Republic envisaged a country divided into two sharply contrasted spaces — Paris and Provinces, corresponding to notions of urban and rural, progressive and conservative, modern and traditional, change and stability. The tendency had existed under the *ancien régime*, with its concentration of court life and political power at Versailles; but it deepened during the nineteenth century, as the country developed industrially, transport improved with the coming of the railways (the network being entirely centered on Paris) and the population of the capital grew out of proportion to that of other cities. The division between modern capital and retarded provinces was further accentuated by political change. In Britain, under a stable political régime, towns like Manchester, Birmingham and Leeds could be seen to possess a sense of their own civic and cultural identity, rival national capitals survived to a greater or lesser extent in Edinburgh, Dublin and Cardiff, and there were rival intellectual centres outside London in Oxford and Cambridge; but in France successive changes of régime (revolutions in 1830 and 1848, Louis Bonaparte's *coup d'état* of 1851), greatly reinforced the understanding that Paris, and Paris alone, was the focus of national power.

The high point of this tendency came with the Paris Commune of 1871, a change of national government that was effectively confined to the capital. During the two periods on either side, the Second Empire and the 'Belle Epoque' of the Third Republic before 1914, Paris was not only the political and intellectual capital of France, but a city with strong claims to being the intellectual and cultural capital of Europe: cosmopolitan, as well as urban and progressive, in contrast to the 'true France' (but at the same time the 'old France') of the provincial towns and *le terroir*. Writers and intellectuals with any ambition at all had to gravitate towards the centre. Zola came up from Provence and, in *Les Rougon-Macquart*, his great novel-cycle which aimed to portray every *milieu* in the society of the Second Empire, ventured outside the capital to depict life in a southern provincial town (*Les Conquête de Plassans*), rural paradise (*La Faute de l'Abbé Mouret*), the idiocy of rural life (*La Terre*) or the misery of a northern mining town (*Germi-*

nal); but more than half the novels in the cycle, and all the ones that deal with major themes like money, politics and art, are set in Paris. Those like Zola's contemporary Alphonse Daudet, who chose to remain in Provence and make it the setting for his work, were inevitably branded 'provincial writers'.

Much the same applies both to the cinema industry and to its product; Marcel Pagnol, who set up a studio outside Paris during the 1930s, is the outstanding exception to the rule. Despite that, the films that he and others made from his work during the decade (e.g., the 'Pagnol trilogy', *Marius*, *Fanny* and *César*) were perceived as rather quaintly Provençal or *marseillais* — and more acutely so, I believe, than the adaptations of his work sixty years later, in Claude Berri's *Jean de Florette* and *Manon des Sources*, or Yves Robert's *La Gloire de mon père* and *Le Château de ma mère*. The society that these later films portrayed belonged to the past, but it was a past that (especially in the last two) might belong to any French family, described with less emphasis on the local peculiarities of the setting and the characters. For a variety of reasons, some of the quaintness and 'otherness' of the world beyond the Parisian *boulevards extérieurs* had been eroded.

There were many reasons for this. During the Second World War, the Vichy régime had tried to reverse the moral significance of the equation: where Paris, progressive, modern and cosmopolitan, had been perceived as superior (if less authentically 'French') than the remainder of the country, Vichy propagandists exalted the 'true France' and the virtues of rural conservatism — for them, 'progressive' and 'cosmopolitan' meant 'communist' and 'foreign' (or, specifically, Jewish), and consequently hostile to the values summed up in the Vichy slogan of 'Work, Family, Fatherland'. The order of the day was the maintenance of catholic family life and honest toil on behalf of the nation, all of which were to be found in the peasant communities of Brittany or the Auvergne more readily than among sophisticated Parisian intellectuals and financiers: hence the outrage among Pétainist critics at the portrayal of provincial life in *Le Corbeau* and the post-war misinterpretation of Louis Daquin's film *Premier de cordée* as Pétainist propaganda, because its depiction of 'man's struggle against nature' seemed to have fascist undertones (compare the 'mountain' films of Leni Riefenstahl).

The Liberation, of course, saw a reaction and, when the provinces feature in the films of the Fourth Republic, it tends to be once more an undefined space, or one defined principally by its difference from the capital. However, developments in camera technology meant that film-makers were becoming less bound to the studio and, though the industry was still centered on Paris, location work outside was a more viable option than it had previously been, meaning that provincial towns could be depicted more easily in specific details of their topography and everyday life. At the same time, the cultural policy of presidents from Georges Pompidou onwards tended towards decentralisation, setting up *centres culturels* outside Paris that became a focus for a host of local activities. By the 1980s, the regional political reorganization under Mitterrand reflected (rather than caused) a genuine shift of power, marked by an upsurge of local or national (Breton, Corsican, Occitan, Basque) feeling and sense of identity. The 'provinces' that Chabrol depicted in *Le Beau Serge* (1958) were already located in a specific place, Sardent, even though its lifestyle was described in contrast to that of Paris as belonging to those who had remained, rather than those who left for the capital. By the time of *Le Boucher*, twelve years later, Sarlat needs no such reference and the 'other' is the one who has left, not those who have stayed behind.

The change is also visible in an adaptation of a story by Simenon that bears some resemblance to *Le Boucher*, Pierre Granier-Deferre's *La Veuve Couderc* (1971). During the 1920s, a lonely woman (Simone Signoret), the widow of the title, who lives on a farm in Burgundy, shelters a criminal (Alain

Delon) and protects him from the police. As in *Le Boucher*, the underlying argument is about love rather than about crime, the woman's readiness to defy conventional morality in sexual relationships being seen as a positive good, regardless even of the man's social worth and the fact that it means circumventing the law. The most striking feature of the film, however, is its precise and affectionate depiction of the Burgundian countryside. The morality of the inhabitants may be merely 'provincial', but they inhabit a real location, with its own customs and history.

In crime films, provincial cities were also acquiring a more recognizable profile: the Marseille of Melville's *Le Deuxième souffle* (1966) is very different from the caricature to be found in Pagnol. In the Resistance movie, *L'Armée des ombres* (1969), Melville went to Lyon, a regional capital that, like Marseille, had a flourishing cultural and social life, largely ignored in the cinema. Lyon was also the location for Bertand Tavernier's *L'Horloger de Saint-Paul* (1973), yet another Simenon adaptation and one which adopts a moral stance comparable to that of *Le Boucher* and *La Veuve Couderc*.

The model of the suspense thriller puts the commission of the crime at the centre of the narrative: in *Du rififi chez les hommes*, for example, the narrative revolves around the mechanics of the robbery, and the central question is whether the perpetrators will succeed in their plans. This, of course, implies an ethical question: as Hitchcock remarked in one of his many reflections on the art of suspense, the audience can be made to hold its breath while the crime is in progress, fearing for the villain, even when its sympathies should properly be against him. There is a good example in Hitchcock's late film *Frenzy* (1972), where a particularly unpleasant killer (played by Barry Foster) is trying to conceal a corpse in a sack of potatoes on the back of a lorry at night in Covent Garden, and the lorry is unexpectedly driven away with the murderer still in it. Our nervousness at this point in the film is a technical one: when a character undertakes a complex and dangerous task, and we have understood the goal, we shall be anxious until it is reached, regardless of whether we see his or her success, in broader terms, as desirable or not. In the same film, when the victims are about to be killed, we share their fear of death (rather than the killer's fear of interruption), our reactions being directed by what the camera chooses to show us — fear on the face of the victim, as opposed to an unexpected visitor approaching up the stairs.

Whether the interruption of an event is welcome or unwelcome to the audience does not, therefore, depend so much on the nature of what is taking place, as on what has preceded and the direction of our sympathies: we do not have to approve in principle of bank robbery to hope that the criminals in *Rififi* will succeed in carrying out their operation, nor do we have to be especially hostile to the murderer in *Le Boucher* to hope that Hélène has succeeded in shutting him out of her house — these things are purely functions of the narrative, like our desire for the crime to be interrupted when it is the 'hero' who is rushing towards the scene. And, while crime provides the most powerful stimulus for these anxieties, it is not the only one: in *Le Salaire de la peur*, notably, the methods of the suspense thriller are employed in a narrative that does not involve any breach of the law (though it is, arguably, a 'crime' that men should have to risk their lives to profit an international company). On the other hand, like the device of 'the least likely suspect', audience anxiety can be directed to particular ideological ends.

In the pure model of the investigative mystery, the crime (or crimes) play a quite different rôle, initiating the enquiry, so that methodology and motivation can be progressively revealed and culminate in the unmasking of the perpetrator. The problem with the classic mystery is plausibility. For uncertainty to persist long enough to sustain our attention, method or motive have usually to be left unclear until the last moment, whereas we know that in real life the how and why of a crime are generally obvious, and the perpetrator is someone with a clear reason and opportunity, not one among a neatly assembled collection of lodgers or the weekend guests at a country house. In actuality, the job of the police consists in constructing a viable case, not in exploring metaphysical problems of motivation or technical puzzles connected with locked rooms.

Chabrol, in *Le Boucher*, uses some techniques of suspense and mystery, but only to sidestep the central premise of either genre. We are not asked to puzzle over the commission of the crimes, we are not left uncertain for very long about the identity of the killer (who turns out to be the only available suspect), and Chabrol employs none of the usual devices to make us wonder whether or not he will be caught. Most of all, he refuses to give any definite answer to the question that we do ask, which is why Popaul commits his crimes; on the contrary, the motives that do suggest themselves (sadism, alienation as a result of his military experiences, sexual desire) are eliminated one by one, until we are left with a metaphysical question about the mystery of human behaviour. The killer is an essentially 'good' man, driven by impulses that are as inexplicable to him as they are to us, to the point where (contrary to every preconception about the criminal in fiction) he is not in any sense defined by his actions.

The crime and the motivation for it are similarly marginal in Bertrand Tavernier's *L'Horloger de Saint-Paul* (1973), where the main character is not the criminal, but his father. The watchmaker (Philippe Noiret) is presented as a thoroughly likeable, law-abiding man, who has brought up his son by himself after his wife left him. The son (Sylvain Rougerie) is the centre of his life, but his love is unrequited. 'Everyone likes me, except him,' the watchmaker tells the police inspector (Jean Rochefort) who is hunting the son for the murder of an industrialist.

Uncovering the young man's motives for the crime thus

takes on the significance of a personal quest rather than a social one (to identify the criminal). Not that this personal investigation is entirely without a social and political dimension, since it takes place against a background of post-1968 politics, which is evoked with the same care as the geographical setting of Lyon. 'Failing to understand your own children, you try to understand other people's,' the police inspector remarks. Where did the father go wrong? Was the child given too much, or was he deprived in some way that the father is unable to fathom? Why does he refuse to speak to his father even after his arrest?

The friendship that develops between the watchmaker and the inspector as they debate these questions at first appears to underline the divorce between the older and younger generation. The lack of comprehension becomes an allegory for the rebellion of the young against de Gaulle's paternalistic régime which in the preceding fifteen years had given France a high level of material prosperity and stability. The crime that the son has committed is the murder of an industrialist; but he does not belong to any organized left-wing group and offers no coherent explanation for his actions. His defence lawyer suggests that, since the industrialist had just sacked the boy's girlfriend, they may be able to present the murder as a crime of passion, but the young man refuses to accept this excuse, telling his lawyer merely that the dead man represented 'everything that I detest'. In the end, at the cost of the understanding that he has developed with the inspector and without himself being able to explain why he does so, the father declares his total solidarity with his son — an act of love and a leap of faith that explains nothing and ties up none of the loose ends. What we are offered in terms of a solution to the dilemmas posed by the film, is a Sartrean existentialist *engagement*, a commitment that can in the end only be an arbitrary response to the meaninglessness of the human condition; so the loving father opts for the son he does not comprehend, against the social order that he does?

Not quite. These films, *Le Boucher*, *L'Horloger de Saint-Paul*, challenge some basic preconceptions of the conventional thriller, to do with motivation and the identity of the criminal, but they do so on the basis of a still more fundamental disagreement over the nature of guilt. The assumption of the investigative mystery is that the criminal will be brought to justice — disorder has been created by the crime and order will be restored by its elucidation. The classic American *film noir* developed cynical variations on this pattern: the criminal may be punished for the wrong crime, the 'good guy' often uses methods that make him indistinguishable from the 'bad guys', the administrators of justice are sometimes corrupt, and the underlying premise of such films is one of an incurable disorder in the human soul. This may also be an assumption made by Chabrol and Tavernier, but with startling variations, amounting to scepticism about the very notion of justice. In *L'Horloger de Saint-Paul*, this is specifically political. The 'natural' sympathy that exists between Noiret and Rochefort, two men of the same background and age, helps to blur the essential difference between them, which at first appears to be based solely on the fact that they stand on opposite sides in the search for the young criminal. But when, after the boy's arrest, Noiret asks whether he will be mistreated, the inspector reassures him by saying that the police brutality he has heard about is 'reserved for Algerians'. It is from this moment that the viewpoint of the two men starts to diverge.

So, too, do the careers of Chabrol and Tavernier. *L'Horloger de Saint-Paul* was the first film of a director whose central preoccupations are social and political: the seeds of the Revolution in *Que la fête commence* (1974), the making of a murderer in *Le Juge et l'assassin* (1975), art and commitment in *Les Enfants gâtés* (1977), colonialism in *Coup de torchon* (1981), black culture in *Mississippi Blues* (1984), the futility of war in *La Vie et rien d'autre*(1989) and the experience of conscripts at the time of the Algerian conflict in the television documentary *La Guerre sans nom* (1991), the work of the drug squad in *L.627* (1992). The concern for historical and topographical accuracy in these films (including the one for television, which confines itself almost exclusively to veterans from the region of Grenoble) derives from a wish to provide positive proof of what the film-maker wants to assert — this is the *where* and the *when*, implying answers to those other, more problematic questions, about *who* and *why*. Tavernier does not suggest that the problems of right and wrong, innocence and guilt, can be solved simply by a Maigret unravelling the puzzle and identifying the agent in the crime. On the contrary, these matters are problematic precisely because they relate back to a whole complex of social and political issues; but, in the light of these, they are capable of solution. The agents are created by forces that we can identify as good or evil: the doctor in *La Guerre sans nom* is not merely a good man, but a good man because he transcended his origins and opted for humanity over obedience to orders.

In Chabrol, an equal attention to *where* and *when* is driven by a contrary sense of the *who* and *why*, and serves only to highlight the impenetrability of questions about identity and motive. The mass murderer Landru, in Chabrol's film of 1962, is not in any way explained by his conventional bourgeois manners or the association that the design of the film makes with nineteenth-century 'decadent' art: he merely coexists with them and kills for some reason that we are left unable to explain. Landru, Robin Wood wrote, 'accepts his world and carries its mercenary values to their monstrous conclusion, retaining at the same time the integrity of a secure, if enigmatic, private identity . . . He accepts his own corruption and the corruption of his world, plunging into mass-murder in order to keep afloat — in much the same spirit as Chabrol, after making this film, was to plunge into a period of purely commercial enterprise, the corrupt world of the spy-genre.' Landru, Wood concludes (perhaps provocatively) was the closest Chabrol had come to self-portraiture!

It is surely unnecessary to go that far. The personal

The Wages of Fear (Le Salaire de la Peur) — 1953

The Wages of Fear (Le Salaire de la Peur) — 1953

Lift to the Scaffold (Ascenseur pour l'Échafaud) — 1957

Shoot the Piano Player (Tirez sur le Pianiste) — 1960

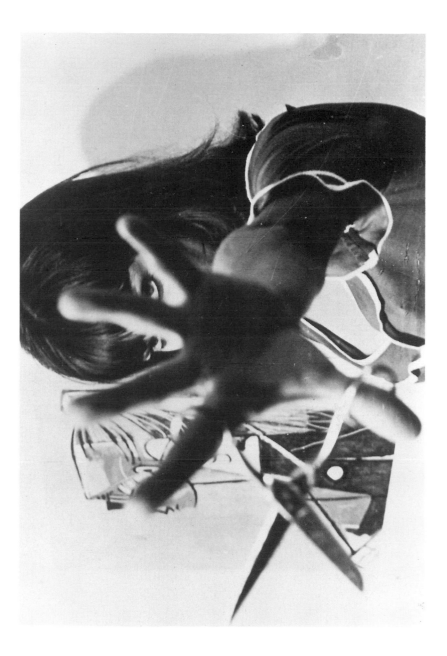

Pierrot le Fou — 1965

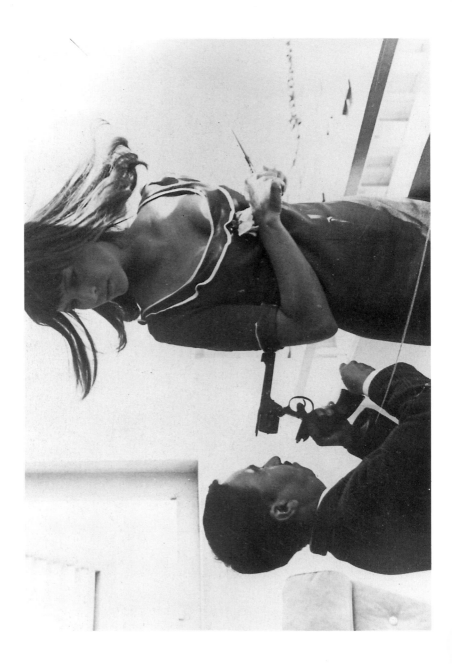

Pierrot le Fou — 1965

Pierrot le Fou — 1965

Pierrot le Fou — 1965

Weekend — 1967

Weekend — 1967

Weekend — 1967

Making It/Going Places (Les Valseuses) — 1974

Making It/Going Places (Les Valseuses) — 1974

Making It/Going Places (Les Valseuses) — 1974

Making It/Going Places (Les Valseuses) — 1974

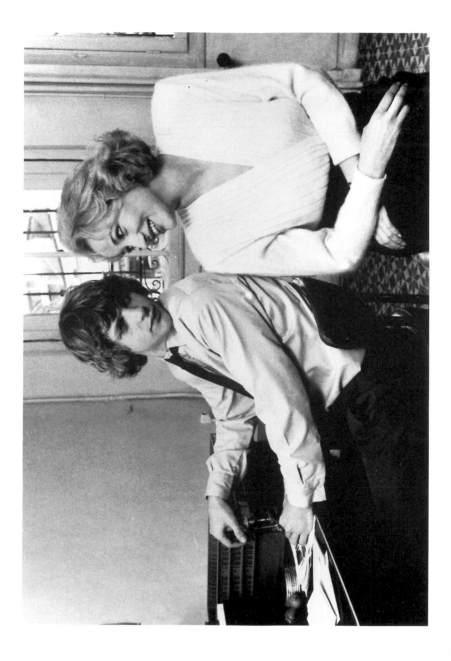

Cop au Vin (Poulet au Vinaigre) — 1984

Police — 1985

Police — 1985

Police — 1985

Police — 1985

Subway — 1985

Mauvais Sang — 1986

The Vanishing — 1988

The Vanishing — 1988

The Vanishing — 1988

Nikita — 1990

Autobus (Aux Yeux du Monde) — 1991

Autobus (Aux Yeux du Monde) — 1991

Autobus (Aux Yeux du Monde) — 1991

L. 627 — 1992

L. 627 — 1992

L. 627 — 1992

element in Chabrol's work following his lapse from Catholicism in the early 1960s lies, surely, in a conviction that there are no final and truthful answers to the questions about identity and guilt. We may try to suggest answers, in the light of sociology, politics or catholic faith, but none of these is the ultimate truth about the person, even if we can be sure that we have identified the guilty party. The Other always keeps his or her secret, and the labels that we apply to motives (greed, egotism, sexual desire, revenge, anger or whatever), only tend to mask our ignorance. The investigative mystery that opens an enquiry then closes it on a 'solution' may satisfy the audience, but cannot satisfy the maker of *Landru*.

What the form of the thriller provides is a space in which one can ask this kind of question; to supply a final answer (Landru was the product of nineteenth-century society, Landru was motivated by greed) is to show that one has misunderstood or evaded the question. This is not to say that all the protagonists in Chabrol's films are morally neutral or morally equal. In *Que la bête meure (1969)*, Paul (Jean Yanne — Popaul from *Le Boucher*) is a thoroughly unpleasant character and we feel that he deserves to be the murder victim that he eventually becomes. The story is taken from the novel by Nicholas Blake (C. Day-Lewis), *The Beast Must Die*, and concerns a man's search for the hit-and-run driver who has killed his son. Chabrol sets his film in Brittany, a location that he once again observes precisely, and makes a highly significant change to the ending of the story. Charles (Michel Duchassoy) identifies Paul as the driver and plans to kill him. When Paul is killed, Charles is arrested, but then Paul's son, Philippe (Marc Di Napoli), who has also been plotting to kill his father, confesses to the murder. Charles is released, before himself leaving a confession, on which the film ends.

We are thus left with an ending that invites us to choose our own solution or to accept that no final solution exists. Did Philippe confess in order to save Charles and purge his own sense of guilt? Did Charles confess to save Philippe? Each of the two is a potential killer, and thus bears a measure of guilt, particularly in Christian terms, and pointing this out may be more important than identifying the actual perpetrator of the crime. Our sympathies, meanwhile, lie with both men, not with the victim, who may himself be more guilty than either of them, since he is incapable of feeling remorse for sacrificing his own interests to those of others. The simple progress from commission of act to identification of agent, with its assumption that an unlawful act means a guilty agent, has been discarded in favour of an open-ended narrative in which guilt can be a property of more than one protagonist.

There is a price to be paid. The model of the closed narrative might be unsatisfactory because of its simplified human dilemmas and questions of motive, or because it took for granted definitions of right and wrong that were ultimately political, cultural and social; but the closed narrative depicting the struggle between good and evil in easily understood terms had a dramatic tension that was in danger of being lost. It is hard to maintain suspense in an audience once it has realized that there will be no final resolution to the problem being posed or which does not know where to place its sympathies. At the end of the road taken by *Les Valseuses* is the 'road movie', all too often a picaresque ramble with nowhere to go; and the open-ended mystery could only too easily lead towards mere mystification. The thriller needed to look for new villains, or to discover some new villainy in the old ones.

V.

POLICE

In 1977, Depardieu took the title role in Francis Girod's comedy *René-la-Canne*. It was a commercial failure, and one would be hard pressed to find reasons why this was undeserved. Depardieu has a characteristic part, as an anarchic petty criminal during the Occupation who persuades a policeman working for the Resistance (Michel Piccoli) to adopt the identity of another crook, to avoid falling into the hands of the Gestapo. At the end of the film, after the Liberation, it is Piccoli who persuades Depardieu to adopt the identity of a policeman so that the two of them can escape with the loot. Sylvia Kristel plays the madam of a brothel who sleeps with both men — but why bother with the intervening plot, which consists mainly in a series of bedroom scenes, interrupted by frenetic chases?

Back to the very start of the film, which shows Depardieu dressed as a German officer, fleeing through the streets of Montmartre on horseback, pursued by the Wehrmacht. 'This young man,' the French public prosecutor says at his trial, 'who, in the words of the Maréchal [i.e. Pétain], preferred self-indulgence to self-sacrifice . . . profaned the uniform — a German uniform; but a uniform is a uniform.' No, we are supposed to reply: a uniform is not a uniform; but it is typical of a right-thinking Pétainist, upholder of law and order at any price, to believe that it is.

For reasons of structure, the investigative mystery usually requires that we should identify the representatives of the law with the law, and the Law itself with justice and right. The narrative starts with the commission of a crime, the creation of a state of disorder which we perceive in the form of questions: *who, why* and (sometimes) *how*? Answering the questions satisfies us by restoring the order that has been disrupted and we side ultimately with the agency that brings this about. When the agent is invariably Maigret or some equivalent representative of the police, the narrative tends to become formulaic; but the devices employed to vary the formula (maverick cop, private eye, insurance investigator, even lone enforcer or vigilante) are seldom more than elegant variations, amounting to an affirmation of the principle that the Law is just, and hence the statement of a desirable order. *La loi, c'est la loi.*

In a country where the political regime has often changed (and with it the legislative authority), it is even reassuring to watch fictional narratives which assert that certain crimes, such as murder, are wrong, regardless of who may be in charge. But the circumstances of the Occupation cast doubt even on this. The Maréchal stood for continuity and the restoration of order after the defeat, and a large number of French people opted for that, though it meant submitting either to direct rule from Germany or rule by a puppet regime. Some refused, and went into hiding to avoid forced labour in Germany or collaboration, joined the Resistance or chose exile and service with the Free French. Those who remained and chose order found themselves obliged to make compromises which, after the Liberation, appeared immoral, in the light of the illegitimacy of the order they had espoused.

In particular, the years after the war saw the gradual uncovering of revelations about the extent to which the French civil police had cooperated with the German authorities, in such matters as the rounding-up of Jews at the Vélodrome d'Hiver in Paris, ready for transportation to the death camps. During the months of the *épuration* immediately after the Liberation, members of the fascist *Milices* and other collaborators were imprisoned or shot, at best after a summary trial. This disorder was widely seen as right and the order it replaced as wrong.

Of course, war itself abolishes the prohibition against killing that applies in peacetime, but it does so in controlled and well-understood circumstances: soldiers kill on behalf of the legitimate state authority. The war film correspondingly differs from the crime film in its approach to the question of good and evil, and the uniform is usually a reliable badge. The failure of the public prosecutor in *René-la-Canne* to perceive this, and to realize that one uniform is not the same as another, consequently indicates a profound corruption in the State itself. He is worse than a venial official, he is the official of a state that is no longer entitled to speak for *la patrie*, and an order that is on the side of a greater disorder. In such circumstances, the petty criminal may come to stand for right.

When Costa-Gavras was making his first film, *Compartiment tueurs*, in 1964, he worked under the sceptical eye of a representative of the Parisian police, who was there less to assist with details of police methods, than to ensure that the results could not be considered detrimental to the good name of the force. The good name? Intolerance of authority goes with *joie de vivre* and verbal wit as part of the average French person's self-image, and there is perhaps no country in Europe where the police have been so generally ridiculed and disliked — in spite of Maigret. The French comic policeman comes in two guises: as the fatuous and narrow-minded character played by Louis de Funès (in *Le Gendarme de Saint-Tropez* and its sequels during the 1970s), or as the likeable, but corrupt manipulator played by Philipe Noiret in *Les Ripoux* (1985). The public could laugh at these caricatures, with an edge of malice, because the image (right-wing, venal, stupid, brutal) was seen as a comic transposition of reality. The authorities were particularly sensitive, too, because of the role played by the police during the Occupation. In Costa-Gavras' film, the censor demanded one alteration in the script, to make the killer's accomplice only a trainee, not a fully-fledged member of the force.

It was typical for Costa-Gavras to start by making a thriller. Konstantinos Gavras, though he was born in Greece and did not arrive in France until 1952, originally as a literature student, from then on followed an established path into the French cinema industry: training at the IDHEC (Institut des Hautes Etudes Cinématographiques) where he studied the different technical disciplines of scriptwriting, editing, synchronization and so on, as well as the practice and theory of directing; then *stagiaire*, working as assistant to Yves Allégret, Jacques Demy, René Clair, René Clément, Marcel Ophuls and others. For Costa-Gavras, as for Louis Malle, a competent genre film was considered a suitable début, and was often the only opening, for a young director.

The same long apprenticeship was undertaken, for example, by Claude Sautet: IDHEC, shorts, assistant, scriptwriter and collaboration with Jacques Becker, then a first film, *Classe tous risques* (1960), which he described to me (1988) as 'a thriller of a kind that did not exist in France at the time . . . a crime film that was heavily influenced by American B-movies, but at the same time very French, with a rhythm of tenderness and violence.' Like many during the 1950s, he had been brought up on American cinema and American literature — which meant Faulkner and Dos Passos, as well as crime fiction. Jean-Paul Rappeneau is another who followed this well-structured road into well-structured films: 'For those of my generation, it was American cinema . . . '

In a country where the centre ground of public opinion was situated well to the left of post-war, capitalist America — the IDHEC itself was part of a state educational system and the French cinema industry has flourished thanks to state, rather than private patronage — the lessons of American popular cinema were technical, rather than ideological. There was often a conflict between admiration for the narrative skills of Hollywood cinema, creating pleasure in the entertainment they provided, and rejection of capitalist or Cold War messages: even Eric Rohmer, the least 'political' of the directors who were to emerge from the New Wave, found that the popularity of Hollywood 'owed more to the devil than to the Almighty', because it relied on the economic power of the United States in the world market; but went on to praise its classicism of form, its efficacy and its elegance (*Cahiers du cinéma*, 54, 1955). American values and the American way of life tended to be taken for granted, as an almost invisible part of the background, by film professionals, who concentrated on form — and perhaps underestimated the powerful appeal of these values to an audience which did not read writers like Dos Passos and Faulkner. In any case, in genre films like the thriller, structural elements dominated, and any ideological message was usually subliminal.

The release of *Rear Window*, Chabrol wrote in *Cahiers du cinéma* in April, 1955, should 'create a united front in film criticism', even convincing those 'Anglo-Saxon' critics who had previously dismissed Hitchcock. There was a large element of self-congratulation in the 'discovery' of Hollywood *auteurs* like Nicholas Ray, Howard Hawks and, above all, Hitchcock — as if to say that French intellectuals had been first to perceive the aesthetic qualities in films that the dull-witted Americans and British were inclined to consider mere entertainment. A prophet is not without honour, save in his own country. The pages of *Cahiers* during the 1950s tend towards exaggerated comparisons, with Greek tragedy, with Renaissance art, as a means of making the point; comparisons that are permitted, because the writers can see beyond the surface elements of story, themes, setting and (in the event) political ideology, because they can overlook the capitalist economics of the industry and its primarily financial objectives and discover the classical efficacy and elegance of form.

The self-awareness of Hitchcock was a particular feature of his appeal: as the director Yves Robert says, he 'manipulates suspense with an irony and mockery that tells you: "we are in this together, *hein*? We are going to laugh at this and be scared by that".' The ordinary cinemagoer only appreciates the manipulation subconsciously and delivers himself, or herself, willingly into the manipulator's hands, ready to laugh or fear on command. The essence, however, is not what we find amusing or frightening, but how these emotions are conveyed. And, once the method is understood, then it can be applied to a variety of ends by film-makers who have been efficiently trained in their craft.

The period of the New Wave gave opportunities to a host of new directors who had not been down the conventional path of IDHEC, followed by years of apprenticeship. Their attitude to the well-made French films of the 1950s was dismissive, and their view of American genre movies was correspondingly different. They did not see them in structural, but in cultural terms, as contributing myths and heroes to an exciting, modern visual environment; and they plundered them accordingly, for fragments in the collage, dislocated meanings, ironies, complicities with audiences that had shared the experience of growing up with Bogart and Monroe and Cagney. The hand-held cameras, location shooting and loose narratives often gave these films a documentary feel, creating a visual affinity with the work of documentarists like Chris Marker and Joris Ivens, who were carrying on traditions of political film-making that looked towards Soviet, not American models.

Enter Costa-Gavras. The son of a Resistance fighter who had been jailed after the war (under anti-communist legislation, though not in fact a communist), Costa-Gavras left Greece to avoid the repercussions of his father's imprisonment. His experience in Greece, plus his apprenticeship in cinema, were to suggest new uses for the genre that he had adopted for his first full-length feature, *Compartiment tueurs*.

Apart from the elements that worried the Paris police, this appeared to be a fairly routine thriller, from a novel by Sébastien Japrisot (Jean-Baptiste Rossi), about a murder on the night express from Marseille to Paris. One interesting feature is that the plot revolves around the elimination of witnesses by the murderers, a standard element in thriller stories, in which truth becomes the goal of a race between investigator and killer, the first trying both to prevent more murders and get to the evidence before it has been erased, the second being driven to kill again and again, in order to conceal his tracks. The race, which is a nightmare for both sides, acts as a device to heighten tension, but it also provides a good model for the political cover-up: the shooting of Lee Harvey Oswald after the Kennedy assassination was still fresh in everyone's mind in 1965.

The film was important for other reasons. Firstly, it introduced Costa-Gavras to Yves Montand who played the police inspector. Secondly, the cameraman, Jean Tournier, was a specialist of *cinéma-vérité*, a style of filming that gave a documentary or newsreel effect. Costa-Gavras used Tournier on his next film, *Un Homme de trop* (1967), a resistance drama set in France. He now had the recipe for the creation of a new genre, the political thriller, the ingredients of which are: the thriller narrative, Hitchcockian suspense, political theme and a sprinkling of lessons from *cinéma-vérité*, documentary and the Italian Neo-Realist works which had led forward to Francesco Rosi's *Salvatore Giuliano* (1961), an immediate precursor of *Z*.

Adapted by Costa-Gavras and Jorge Semprun from the novel by Vassilis Vassilikos, *Z* is set in an unnamed country and Yves Montand plays an unnamed political figure; but the events are patently based on the assassination of the Greek politician Gregory Lambrakis, in May 1963. It was originally to have been funded by United Artists, but they pulled out when they saw the script. Costa-Gavras hunted for another production company, finally getting the money from a French producer and from the Algerian national film company, which also provided the locations for filming (the story could not, for obvious reasons, be shot in Greece).

The plot, told largely in flashback, concerns the killing of 'Z' (Yves Montand), a pacifist deputy and doctor, after a political meeting, followed by attempts to prove that his death was caused deliberately and not, as the authorities pretend, by a traffic accident. Behind the immediate assassins, the investigation reveals a conspiracy that goes to the heart of government. But, even though the truth is finally revealed, the film departs from the conventions of the thriller by rejecting the comforting assumption that justice has triumphed. The ending evokes the Greek colonels' coup of 1967 and gives a list of things that they have banned, including the music of Mikis Theodorakis, who composed the score for the film, and the letter 'Z', the first letter of the Greek word for 'he lives'.

Claude Veillot, in *L'Express*, called *Z* 'the first French political film' — though the description was rejected by Costa-Gavras, who preferred 'adventure film'. In fact, most critics noted the thriller elements, Pauline Kael saying that *Z* derived 'not from the traditions of the French film but from American gangster movies and prison pictures and anti-fascist melodramas of the forties', done in 'modern movie style' (*New Yorker*, December 13, 1969). Costa-Gavras' achievement was to show how this formal structure of the thriller could be applied to a political story, largely by a change of motive: *Z*'s real killers were driven by the desire for political power, not sex or money. The discovery was not, in itself, entirely new: power had always been one motive, at least, in gangster films, and documentary elements had been introduced into the genre in G-men movies or others that attempted to take the lid off the naked city, with location shooting and attention to details of police procedure — the prime example being Jules Dassin's *The Naked City* (1948) itself.

The difference, in the case of *Z*, is that the film's message was explicitly directed against a corrupt, right-wing government. American films had shown small-scale or small-town corruption and may, at a stretch, have implied that power-hungry mobsters were analogous to politicians (they like to have city hall in their pockets) or businessmen (whose legal status they covet); during the Cold War years, spy thrillers had attacked the methods of totalitarian regimes. But *Z*, filmed in colour and addressed to a generation that obtained its news increasingly through television, enrolled the techniques of thriller and documentary to warn against the persistent threat from an old enemy, the right. The devil who came out of the sky in *Triumph of the Will* was not yet defeated, and this was a message that the late 1960s were willing to hear.

The impact of the film was considerable, although there were many on both sides of the political divide who questioned its political credentials, mainly because they found the mixture of popular genre and serious content suspect: Emile Breton, in his update for Georges Sadoul's *Dictionnaire des films*, accuses it of ambivalence, reducing a political struggle purely to the mechanism of a conspiracy. Perhaps 'conspiracy thriller' is the best description, suggested in retrospect by the film's successors, like *All the President's Men*, *Silkwood* and, most recently, Oliver Stone's *JFK*. The atomic age, understandably, if often against its will, has been obsessed with conspiracies: during the Cuba crisis, the fate of the world had been in the hands of two men with their fingers on the nuclear trigger, so the spy thriller version of political struggle, reducing conflict to the level of a few men in government and their agents, secret, conspiratorial, coming down ultimately to the sole question of whether James

Bond could foil Dr No or Rosa Klebb, was persuasive. Even the cynical spy thriller made the same basic assumptions, while casting the agents (Harry Palmer and others who tried to come in from the cold) as themselves victims of a tiny group of unelected, largely uncontrolled manipulators, implying that in Western democracies politicians had become, at least partly, front men, manipulated from behind the scenes, or the victims in struggles that were being determined outside the ostensible structures of state power. Z opens with a litany of mysterious assassinations: Jack Kennedy, Robert Kennedy, Malcolm X, Mehdi Ben Barka, Patrice Lumumba, Enrico Mattei, Humberto Delgado. A single shot might prove more decisive than a million votes.

The attraction of Maoism was that it contradicted the received version of international politics, and argued that peasants on bicycles could take on, and defeat, the army of the greatest superpower. While America and the Soviet Union were engaged in their conspiratorial global conflict, the Vietcong and other Third World guerilla armies were demonstrating that the struggle between rival ideologies might still be determined by a people's war. Thus the battlelines were redrawn, between those who accepted the official version of the struggle and those who rejected it. The latter group were inclined to see Costa-Gavras' film as a study of the mechanism, not the underlying causes.

In reality, as his next three films were to show, Costa-Gavras was concerned less with political ideologies than with political justice. *L'Aveu* (1970), *Etat de siège* (1973) and *Section spéciale* (1975) deal successively with the Stalinist show trials in Czechoslovakia, the 'popular justice' meted out by South American guerilas to a CIA agent and the French judiciary under the German occupation. Each film was based on real events and each, predictably, drew criticism from those who had some ideological investment in a particular interpretation of history. The criticism was sometimes merely dismissive ('anti-communism' or 'anti-Americanism' in the case of the first two), but was more often formulated in aesthetic terms: 'stereotyping' and 'over-simplification'. As with the related genre of drama-documentary, Costa-Gavras' political fictions were open to attack from opposite directions: either they were misleading because they sacrificed the facts to the demands of a good story, or else they were dull because the narrative was overburdened with facts.

Costa-Gavras returned to the (political) thriller in *Betrayed* (1988) and *Music Box* (1989), the first starring Debra Winger as an undercover agent investigating a murder by American white supremacists, the second with Jessica Lange as the daughter of a suspected war criminal. Both are American films, so outside the scope of this book, though they share the conventional thriller's concern with problems of identity and justice, asking Hitchcockian questions about the nature of guilt, and how well we know the people we love. But, where the conventional thriller examines these problems in the context of domestic drama, the Costa-Gavras thrillers apply them to actual historical events and situations. The purpose may be to clarify a complex political argument and enhance it with the appeal of a fictional narrative (suspense, characterization, structure), but the effect is also to reveal political elements (in the broadest sense) that were already present in the adopted genre.

The French understanding of the relationship between the state and the individual was conditioned during the post-war period by the events of the Occupation and by costly defeats in the colonial wars in Indochina and Algeria. The concession of independence to France's other former colonies in Africa, during the early years of the Fifth Republic, confirmed the end of the country's imperial role. Despite the Gaullist stance of partial non-alignment, despite the nuclear *force de frappe*, despite the European Community and growing prosperity, there was no disguising the fact that France had become relatively more marginal in world affairs, whether one located the central issue here in the Cold War between the superpowers or in the struggles of the Third World; and it can be argued, as Jill Forbes does in *The Cinema in France*

After the New Wave, that the cinema industry, and crime films in particular, by defining themselves in relation to Hollywood and Hollywood genres, had long recognized this marginality. The two watershed years of 1958 (de Gaulle's assumption of power) and 1968 (the radical challenge to his regime) had a profound effect on mentalities. And, if the state is the guardian of justice, these challenges to its authority raised questions about the political implications of even non-political 'crimes'. The switch from conformism to *contestation* of the central character in *L'Horloger de Saint-Paul* is a watchmaker's adjustment to changing times.

It was not a simple change from blind belief to clear-eyed cynicism. On the contrary, the watchmaker relinquishes certainties founded on a reasoned view of the world to a solidarity with his son that is irrational and emotional. While there had always been, even in the fatalism of the pre-war Carné-Prévert films, an underlying sense of the difference between true justice and the justice of the courts — the Platonic idea and the imperfect reality — the implication was that nothing could be done to change this aspect of the human condition, and Carné's post-war successors came to broadly the same conclusion. It is the sardonic ending that establishes the ethos of *Le Salaire de la peur*, not its references to the exploitation of the characters by American capitalism or the passing evocation of the still more abject poverty of the Indians who sit, in attitudes of wise resignation, by the side of the road: the film is a fable, divorced from present reality by being set in an anonymous South American country, which the men do not aim to change, but to leave. Their ambition, to earn enough money to return to Europe and live in modest comfort in their own countries, removes us definitively from the site of any political action and the final twist to the plot tells us that we are all in the same situation, lulled by false hopes, feverishly working towards a future that can have only one outcome.

The doomed Gabin of the Carné-Prévert films comes back as the older Gabin of *Touchez pas au grisbi*, a criminal longing to escape into retirement, but foiled by circumstances. Fate pursues the lovers of Becker's *Casque d'or*, the killers in Clouzot's *Les Diaboliques*, the thieves of Dassin's *Du rififi chez les hommes*, the murderer of Malle's *Ascenseur pour l'échafaud* and the wild tearaways played by Belmondo in Godard's *A bout de souffle* and *Pierrot le fou*. It is heredity, or some impulse, innate and hence equivalent to a form of destiny, that drives *Le Boucher*, not the environment of the Army or the village that he left to join up. In film after film, the central characters are defeated, not by efficient police work or some inevitable outcome of their crimes, but by chance.

There may be a number of reasons for this. One is that the intervention of chance is useful in creating suspense; another that a certain cynicism is part of the genre. Characters who are the victims of fate also attract our sympathy and help to create that moral ambivalence that distinguishes this kind of thriller from police or detective stories in which good and bad are clearly delineated. All these tend to be incompatible with a political message. Politics implies that change is possible, while a view of the human condition that sees us as victims of fate does not; and divided sympathies are no stimulus to political action. The classic *film noir* uses politics only to reinforce disillusionment and cast doubt on motivation, not as a call to arms.

Gangster films had always posited the existence of an alternative code, both of morality and of justice. The protagonists of *Touchez pas au grisbi* are defined as 'good' or 'bad', not with reference to the existing law (according to which, as criminals, they are all 'bad'), but in relation to their own sub-code of loyalty and fair dealing. On the surface, this may appear to constitute a simple alternative society, a kind of allegory for society itself, in which theoretically any set of rules might apply provided it was internally consistent, and any behaviour that conformed to the rules would be 'good', regardless of how it would be judged by the norms of conventional morality. But it is clear that this is only partly the case with a film like *Grisbi*: our sympathies are gained for the central character, not because he obeys his own set of rules, but because his fundamental values are those of conventional morality. Max (Jean Gabin) sacrifices his own interests to save his friend, he keeps his word and he believes in fair dealing. In addition to this, he represents order against anarchy, and is driven to go to war, not because he likes war for its own sake, but because he recognizes the need to preserve a form of social order against the chaos of egotism and naked power. Our inclination to accept that any set of rules is better than none is reinforced by our recognition that Max's code is fair.

The 'Mafia film' takes the premises of the gangster film and transposes them onto a different plane. We know that the Mafia exists, with its 'families' and its code of honour, taking slightly different forms in Sicily, in Naples, in Corsica, in Marseille or in the United States, but real, nonetheless. Unlike the plain gangster film, one about the Mafia is consequently more difficult to read as pure allegory or metonym: even though we may be tempted to see it as a figure for society, it constantly draws us back to the wider context of society itself, and suggests that we interpret the actions of the characters, regardless of whether or not they are consistent with an internal code of honour, as criminal. Our feelings about the central characters are inherently ambivalent and, if we are to sympathize with them (something which is usually essential to sustain interest), our sympathies have to respond to rather different appeals from the ones used by Melville and Gabin in *Grisbi*.

Take the character of Michael Corleone, played by Al Pacino in the American classic of the genre, Francis Ford Coppola's *The Godfather* (1971). Michael is the white sheep of the Family, laundered by a college education, a fine war record and a determination to follow a more socially acceptable line of business than his father and brothers. These good intentions are undermined by the family loyalty that emerges when the Corleones become involved in a 'war' and by the murder of his Italian wife after he 'makes his bones' and goes to escape the heat in Sicily. In other words, we are led to perceive Michael as essentially a 'good' man, who takes a very American decision to put loyalty to his family above the law, and is driven deeper into crime by grief and anger — a victim of fate, in fact, who retains a good measure of our sympathy even in his descent into crime, because we understand and identify with his motives.

More than that: we admire his qualities of heroism, courage and coolness under fire. To begin with, as the white sheep, he is treated by his brothers with a mixture of protectiveness and mild contempt — the 'college boy' whose scruples make him too weak to function effectively in their world, despite his military record in the Second World War. But, when the gang war begins, Michael is the only member of the family able to carry out the assassination of the rival family bosses, and he proves to have all the qualities needed for the *capo di famiglia* that he will eventually become. At this point, we are largely on his side and inclined to interpret the subsequent story of his corruption as an indictment of society, rather than of Michael himself — which helps to achieve Coppola's aim of making the Mafia a figure for American capitalism, even though it refers to an actual criminal organization that is, in reality, at war with American society.

In short, there are two main devices that can be used to induce a willing suspension of hostility towards these inherently unpleasant and violent characters: knowing how the personality was formed, by social background or other circumstances that constitute the character's destiny (again, *tout comprendre, c'est tout pardonner*); and a readiness to give more weight to the virtues demanded by the particular circumstances of the film than to faults that would be reprehensible outside them. These virtues tend to be military ones — something else that underlines the similarity between the genres of gangster and war film. In war, murder may be heroic, so the qualities that make a good murderer (nerve, bravery, resource) gain in value, while love, sympathy, understanding and fairness are devalued.

In the self-referential world of the cinema, it is not even necessary always to establish background and character within the confines of a film: Jean Gabin, Lino Ventura and Eddie Constantine brought expectations with them to every new part, and so did the two leading stars of Mafia films during the 1960s and 1970s, Alain Delon and Jean-Paul Belmondo. Delon's screen persona was established in three films for Melville: as the hired killer of Le *Samouraï* (1967), as the criminal in *La Cercle rouge* (1970) and as the policeman in *Un flic* (1972); the image was cold, rather expressionless, calculating, tough. Belmondo, always carrying some of the free-wheeling spirit of *A bout de souffle* and *Pierrot le fou*, was more hare-brained, funnier, with less sinister undercurrents. Their sex appeal was the excitement that they seemed to represent — Belmondo leaning slightly more towards madcap adventure, Delon more unpredictable and dangerous. Where Belmondo was unambiguously virile, Delon's persona, less athletic, more intellectual and self-sufficient, could suggest both frigidity and sexual ambivalence.

They came together in two period gangster movies, *Borsalino* (1969) and *Borsalino et cie* (1974), directed by Jacques Deray and set in the Marseille underworld of the 1930s. The decade itself had a sort of ambivalent appeal: France in the 1970s was enjoying a passion for *le rétro*, which extended to styles of dress, furniture, architecture, literature, art and design. The films were named after the type of hat worn by the two characters, and the 1930s theme is developed in the design of decor and cars.

It is important to emphasize that the interest was not in history, but in style: *le rétro* is about icons, the power of which is enhanced by displacement. The decade of the 1930s in France has contradictory meanings, according to one's place in the political spectrum. For the left (the generation of 1968), these were the years of the Spanish Civil War and the

Popular Front, the birth of a struggle against fascism that took place against a background of government corruption and financial scandals; the ruling class of the pre-war decade was well-prepared to lapse into the passive or active collaboration of the Occupation years. In fact, during the Occupation fashions in dress and design were artificially frozen, underlining a continuity between the hidden corruption of the pre-war rich and their open corruption in the years of the Milices, the black market, parties with the Occupier and women slipping into bed with officers of the Wehrmacht.

The novels of Patrick Modiano (who wrote the screenplay for Louis Malle's *Lacombe Lucien*) explore this atmosphere of decadence and betrayal. For those who did not see the 1930s and 1940s primarily in ideological terms, the *rétro* style had a peculiarly fetishistic allure, at once dangerous and appealing, which made it subversive with respect to the orthodoxies of the 1970s: compare the use of Nazi insignia by heavy metal and rock bands. Lifted out of their original context and transferred to a contemporary one, hats, jackets, ties, cars, ornaments and so on, acquired an ironic and ludic dimension, playful, stylish and sexy, in the way that dressing up is playful, style means self-awareness and sex involves role-play and games. The violence of films like *Borsalino* is much like the violence of sado-masochism in a brothel, where costumes and instruments of torture are part of a consenting (and, in that context, pleasurable) ritual.

The problem of evil is crucial to classic *film noir*, justice to the political thriller, meaning itself to the post-modernist one. Of course, the relationship of the French crime movie to other literary and cinema traditions had always meant a certain degree of imitation or quotation: there were English literary models for the thrillers of the 1930s, American ones for the early post-war ones and conscious ironies in some, like the Lemmy Caution series, which Jill Forbes explains in terms of the cultural hegemony of America during the post-war period, a love-hate relationship which she characterizes as 'one of tension perceptible in an elaborate intertextuality', the thriller or *polar,* in particular, becoming 'a crucial means through which the relationship between the French cinema and the American was articulated'. But the relationship was never entirely one-way. Even if American audiences were largely unaware of foreign cinema, film-makers were not, and the Americans have borrowed freely from France since the New Wave, both in the form of re-makes, and in more subtle kinds of quotation. The same has been still more true of the British: Maurice Cam's thriller *Métropolitan* (1938), a story about a murder witnessed from a métro train on an overground section of track, was re-made almost immediately as *A Window in London* (Herbert Mason, 1939), using the overground section of the London tube. The original film was described by *The Times* (in 1946) as 'typically French'.

French directors used more or less oblique references to American cinema, to satisfy audience expectations of what a particular type of film should be and how its characters should behave; this may, if one wants, have the effect of 'articulating the relationship' with the source of these elements. There was also, among young critics and directors during the 1950s, a dissatisfaction with French cinema and a tendency to treat the Hollywood product as a model. However, one can exaggerate the significance both of the preference for American films and the use of elements from them. The films of Jean-Luc Godard are littered with books, but this does not make them 'literary'; the books are there as signs, to complicate, to distract, to allow a variety of 'readings', and the references to American cinema serve the same function. The effect of this 'elaborate intertextuality' is, in fact, to create films that are in many ways precisely the opposite of American B-movies, diffuse instead of concentrated, void of narrative, character, suspense and most of the stylistic elements that characterize Hollywood B-movies and *film noir.*

All the elements are present in Godard's *Détective* (1985): a group of stereotypical characters (detective, boxer, boxing manager, Mafia, girlfriends, nymphette) meet in a Paris hotel to investigate an old murder, in a film starring the rock idol Johnny Hallyday, New Wave actor Jean-Pierre Léaud, old hands Alain Cuny and Claude Brasseur, young star Nathalie Baye, theatre actor Laurent Terzieff; and dedicated to John Cassavetes, Clint Eastwood and Edgar G. Ulmer (director of *The Black Cat, Detour, Strange Illusion, Murder Is My Beat, Naked Dawn* and other quickies of the 1930s, 40s and 50s). Full of jokes and in-jokes, virtually plotless, sporadically comic or mysteriously menacing, the movie plays with this bric-a-brac from the Hollywood attic. Movie buffs liked it well enough (Tony Rayns, of the British magazine *Time Out*, called it a 'mini-masterpiece') and it pretty well bears out the notion that the genre, having started as tragedy, was repeating itself as farce. In case we may have overlooked where the movie is coming from, Godard ensures that the chest of drawers in the hotel bedroom is piled high with volumes in the instantly recognizable livery of the *Série noire*, and (in case we have failed to notice them) there is a moment in the film where these are pointedly scattered across the floor. Well, did you get it this time?

We did, thanks. Was that all?

VI.

SÉRIE NOIRE

The argument that the influence of American *film noir* in
France is mainly about articulating France's relationship
with the United States, suggests a willingness to underesti-
mate the extent to which all cultures are both 'impure' and
interdependent. The 'classic', essentially American thriller
was crucially shaped by the contribution of European directors (Hitchcock, Fritz Lang, Robert Siodmak, Billy Wilder,
Otto Preminger, even Edgar G. Ulmer) and by a writer,
Raymond Chandler, who was educated in Europe; as well as
by the visual style of German expressionism, from which its
origins could be traced back to different strands in European
romanticism, including the gothic novel (so, for that matter,
to the gothic novels of the American Charles Brockden
Brown or the tales of Edgar Allen Poe . . .). The part played
by European directors is not irrelevant or coincidental,
because the films that they made were, at least in part, a
critique of American society, expressing precisely those
things which an outsider would feel: alienation, the excite-

ment and danger of the city, its anonymity, the rootlessness of its inhabitants, the central characters' search for identity, and lives at the mercy of impersonal forces, evil, violence and fate.

Moreover, the pessimism of these films and their treatment of sexual relationships made them seem un-American to critics at the time. The time, remember, was the 1940s, when the country was fighting a war against Germany and preparing for a war against Communism. Whichever way you viewed them, German refugees from Nazism were suspect. There were socially aware, left-wing films in the 1940s, some written and directed by Americans, but few coming into the category that would now be labelled *film noir*; if the B-movies had a political message, it was covert. Not so covert, however, as to fool the House Committee on Un-American Activities: 'Where you see something that makes every Senator, every businessman, every employer a crook and which destroys our belief in American free enterprise and free institutions, that is communistic,' according to the scriptwriter, Robert Hughes. The image of the capitalist United States as a haunt of gangsters and petty villains was not one that true Americans wanted to see. Whatever else they may have been, the 1940s thrillers were not 'good American stories'.

This is partly why they appealed so strongly to European audiences as cynical views of an urban jungle that was also the future for Europe: the appeal of American culture in the post-war years had that ambivalence. If you wanted to be modern, you adopted it, including a measure of its own disillusionment with itself. By the 1960s, the attitude was tinged with nostalgia: the future had become future-in-the-past, part of an adolescent experience for the young adults of the New Wave. When they referred to it, it was not as an American reality, but as something integrated into the French past and naturalized as thoroughly as the on-screen films of Giuseppe Tornatore's *Cinema Paradiso* (1988). The young man (Patrick Dewaere) who apes the actions of

American cinema gangsters in the credit sequence of Alain Corneau's *Série noire* (1979) does not illustrate the influence of American movies, but defines himself in relation to French society — specifically, as a marginal, who has lost his sense of identity.

Let's be clear about this: Corneau's generation grew up with America as a significant (and usually attractive) offering on the shelves of the world cultural supermarket. Many enjoyed American or American-style thrillers, some went to university and took degrees in English literature which included a quite large element of American studies. Corneau himself became a semi-professional jazz musician and played with the US 76th Army Band in Orléans, before coming to Paris to study at IDHEC, then lived for a time in New York. *Série noire* is adapted from a novel by the writer Jim Thompson, *A Hell of a Woman*, and Corneau's work as obviously contains elements of the American B-movie as Godard's or Truffaut's; so nothing could be simpler than to classify it — and its *auteur* — as evidence of the penetration of American culture in France.

How does Corneau see it? 'There is only one culture,' he said in a 1979 interview with Yves Alion for *L'Avant-scène du cinéma* (233),'which is bourgeois culture, because the bourgeoisie holds power. Bourgeois culture has always played a politically very ambiguous role, but one which is beneficial in quite a few ways. Since the bourgeoisie is constantly challenging it, we have first of all to struggle to defend what this culture has gained. We shall achieve nothing by all becoming illiterate.'

The most striking thing about this, regardless of precisely what Corneau says, is that, in the context of a discussion on political and aesthetic practice, and socialist realism, these are so obviously the words of a French intellectual of the 1970s: if the same statement had been made by an American film director, he would at once be classified as unusually 'political', probably an independent, certainly someone with a 'European' rather than an American outlook. And, while the cinematic 'language' of *Série noire* quotes from American *film noir*, the element in the film which has attracted most attention is precisely the one that is most obviously and explicitly French, namely the language.

The use of language is intended to reveal the disorder of the central character's personality: as Jill Forbes writes: ' . . . he cannot consistently embrace any one form of language and instead switches register and dialect according to the identity of the interlocutor or the identity he himself is attempting to assume.' The dialogues were written by Georges Perec, an outstanding and characteristic figure in the literature of the 1970s, one of a number of writers around this period who were exploring the possibilities of a new classicism, rebelling against laxity and facility, and experimenting with extraordinarily complex and demanding literary forms. Perec himself was the author of a lipogrammatic novel, *La Disparition*, written entirely without using the letter 'e', and of a marvellous and intricate masterpiece, *La Vie, mode d'emploi*. More immediately relevant to the script of *Série noire* was his first novel, *Les Choses* (1965), about a young couple who seek to find their identity in clichés of language and lifestyle, victims of fashion, advertising and the pursuit of material substitutes for inner meaning.

The language used by Frank (Patrick Dewaere) in *Série noire* is not the hardboiled style developed for the translations in the original series of thrillers, but a compound of that slang with *le verlan* (the 'back slang' of the younger generation during the 1970s and 1980s), the 'blue' language which had also become more usual in films (like *Les Valseuses*) since the relaxation of censorship, everyday street talk, plus fragments of English and elements of standard, even rather high-flown French (*'c'est une histoire d'amour, une terrible histoire d'amour'*). Frank naturally drinks whisky, which he describes as *'du calva d'Ecosse . . . sacoche viski, madine chocotte lande'* ['made in Scotland' — but *avoir les chocottes* means 'to be afraid'] ' . . . *ze velours of ze estomaque.*' He addresses the Greek, Tikides, as *'Zorba de mes couilles'* ('Zorba of my balls') and has a wealth of expressions for women, girls, sexual intercourse, guns, etc. There are times when Perec's script appears almost too clever by half.

In contrast to his 'corrupt' use of language, Frank has a mania for cleanliness that is the cause of the argument with his wife, Jeanne, which could be seen as the motor for the tragic events of the film. The sense of alienation is intensified by the location: the film takes place mainly in Frank's dingy apartment or in a desolate wasteland between tower blocks. Frank is a door-to-door salesman who falls for a prostitute (another stock character) and kills an old woman for her money (compare *Crime and Punishment*). Whether his motivation is love (as he sees it), or greed (as his employer, Staplin, sees it) — indeed, whether he has any real motivation at all — remains unclear. Music plays a major role: Duke Ellington, contemporary pop (Sheila, Claude François) and nostalgic references to Gilbert Bécaud.

Within its own frame of reference, *Série noire* thus implies an indictment of cultural deprivation and alienation, the central character a suburban Bogart ('*Bogart de banlieue*', Gilbert Rochu, *Libération*, April 25, 1979) or the Hamlet of Nanterre (François Chalais, *Le Figaro*, May 17, 1979). 'The speech of the characters in the film,' Corneau said, 'always has its starting-point in cliché' ('. . . *à partir d'une base de lieux communs*') — the key notion being that this is only a starting-point. 'The challenge was to give an appearance of naturalism, but at all costs to avoid succumbing to it: we had to do something totally unrealistic . . . Every phrase is turned around and used obliquely . . . ' The effect is comparable, perhaps, to the songs of Georges Brassens, written in a language that is a mixture of slang and archaism, alternately vulgar and erudite. It is a dialect that, far from suggesting deprivation, asserts the richness of the resources on which it can draw.

If *Série noire* is interpreted as the portrait of 'a histrionic . . . constantly trying out new registers and new commonplaces to ward off disintegration' in a failed attempt 'to fix his personality in and through language' (Jill Forbes), then one must admit the paradox that a character who has access to such a range of language and registers, in a film that makes such knowing use of them, demonstrates precisely the opposite of cultural impoverishment. Translation and transposition are not acts of mere imitation. The language created for the translations in the original *série noire*, which meant finding a French equivalent for an American slang that was itself partly an artificial, literary construct, took on its own meanings in the French context: racy, exotic, subversive and appealing.

The language of a film is clearly the element that will have least significance for a foreign audience. Translated into subtitles, the dialogue can achieve only an approximation of its original resonance (the constraints of subtitling are more rigorous than those of literary translation, for example), with the result that even a film like *Série noire* may appear, not as a transformation, but as an attempt merely to reproduce American models in a French setting. A Frenchman (Belmondo in *A bout de souffle* or *Pierrot le fou*, Dewaere in *Série noire*), modelling himself on Humphrey Bogart, means something different from Bogart dubbed into French — an acknowledgement, certainly, of the influence of Hollywood cinema, but also an assertion of the character's freedom to assimilate this influence. The reason that audiences admire and try to imitate stars is that, while ordinary actors appear to be imprisoned in the texts that they perform, the quality of stardom confers a power over the text, an ability to be simultaneously oneself and the character that one is playing: it is not the fictional character (say, Philip Marlowe) that Belmondo and Dewaere imitate, but the Bogart who can be the character and, through it, externalize his desires.

There is a comparable ambivalence in language to which translation gives a kind of ironic distance. These fictional characters who adopt Hollywood styles and Americanized language, far from demonstrating their subjection to a foreign culture, assert their freedom from the constraints of

French society, from the norms of their native language, from class and background. They extend the possibilities of what it means to be 'French'. This was the role of American culture, particularly cinema culture, throughout Europe in the post-war years: as much in Britain, for example, where the working-class youth of the 1950s adopted American clothes, rock'n'roll, slang and mannerisms, as symbols of rejection of a class system that would condemn them to routine jobs and an inferior social status, confirmed by education, accent and language. To the establishment in these countries, American culture came as a colonizer, resisted in France particularly on the terrain of language and the struggle against *le franglais*; but to those outside the establishment, the effect was liberating.

In France, by the late 1970s, when *Série noire* was made, the language of the genre had progressed from the Simonin argot of the 1950s, to the more Americanized slang of the 1960s, taking on the sexually explicit slang of the younger generation of this and the following decade. It contained a number of terms that could be described (or dismissed) as *franglais*, though gallicized with a facility that 'standard French' found hard to match. A typical snatch of Frank's dialogue illustrates some components of the mixture: '*Ecoute, Tikides, on y va, on se farcit la fillette, on casse tout dans la baraque et pis [puis] on met les bouts, d'accord? . . . allez, on y go . . .* ' [broadly: 'Listen, T., let's go, we'll have the girl, wreck the joint, then get out of there, okay? Come on, let's go'] — standard colloquialisms (the use of the pronoun *on*, the phrase *on y va*), the more emphatically slangy *baraque* and *mettre les bouts*, and the vulgar *se farcir*, followed by an anglicism (*on y go*), a variant on the earlier *on y va*, with obvious ironic force. Developed in a marginal and culturally unacceptable genre, drawing on the language of everyday life which nourished it, and by which it was nourished, this language of the *film noir/polar/*thriller/gangster film, far from declining over the decades, had been constantly enriched. Where a purist in the 1950s might have dismissed the dialogues of the Lemmy Caution films — where every foul-up is *une salade*, every woman *une poupée* ('a doll') to be addressed as *mon sucre* ('sugar') or *p'tite soeur* ('little sister') — as hackneyed and debased, here was evidence that the register had not been condemned to progressive impoverishment.

Perec's script for *Série noire* is, of course, a special case. Even so, this dialect was flourishing: almost every film, whether or not it belonged to the genre, contained elements of it, because of its contribution to the everyday language, particularly of the young. The attitudes and clothes that people imitated from the cinema might be American, but the language was French, even if it was *super-cool* as well as *branché* (or, in back-slang, *chébran*). In short, the effect of Hollywood-style films on a French audience was not to produce a mimicry of Hollywood style, but a new variety of French.

The cinema culture itself was different in France, where old movies were treated with greater respect, even in the 1950s, and recycled through the Cinémathèque and the *Cinémas d'art et d'essai*. During the 1950s, Corneau said (*L'Avant-scène du cinéma*, 233), 'there was a major French *cinéma noir* which, because of the New Wave, was competely forgotten . . . ' Not completely. The New Wave, particularly Truffaut and Godard, had delighted in the pure American thriller, and (in Godard's case) in the potential of the despised French B-movies that imitated it: there were hints of nostalgia and subversion here, challenging the notion of high culture and asserting the virtues of popular taste. The 1970s explored the possibility of the political thriller, either as a new genre (Costa-Gavras) or as a variant on the police procedural. But the mainstream French *film noir* or *polar* (*Grisbi, Les Diaboliques, Rififi*) was still available to cinéastes, cinemagoers or television viewers, and it was time to rediscover its strengths.

However, there was some other business which needed to be got out of the way first. This was to work through the arguments of the New Wave and post-New Wave, much as Godard was doing in *Détective*. The decade of the 1980s opened with a remarkable début film, Jean-Jacques Beineix's *Diva* (1981), bringing together elements from *film noir*, gangster films and old-fashioned serials (Feuillade and the rest) in a concoction that felt, looked and sounded entirely modern. The plot, so far as there is one, concerns a messenger obsessed with a singer (Wilhelminia Wiggins Fernandez) who becomes enmeshed in an obscure tale of corruption and violence. The film dazzled its audiences by giving them everything that they expected from a contemporary thriller: stylish music, stylish photography, stylish editing. The vacuity of style without content was more evident in Beineix's next film, *La Lune dans le caniveau* (1983), adapted from a novel by David Goodis about a worker hunting for the man who has driven his sister to suicide. Gérard Depardieu and Nastassia Kinski starred and, with these leading players and the reputation that Beineix could carry over from *Diva*, the film should have been a success. In fact it was booed at Cannes and did badly at the box office. Depardieu called it 'an idiotic movie' and accused Beineix of making films only to please himself.

Beineix's generation had at its disposal an audience educated by cinema, television, pop videos and the computer, with an allegedly short attention span, but able to read images far more efficiently than its elders had done and pick up clues about fashion, attitudes and behaviour without the screenwriter and director having to spell them out. The 1980s were also a time of technical advance: the 'moving image' was considered to be the main form of communication in the late twentieth century, but hitherto neglected (and dangerously despised) by political and educational establishments still nostalgic for the written word. Parents who saw their children becoming competent in the use of technologies that they did not understand were easily persuaded that the culture had not only changed, but shifted definitively from one base (the written word; or, in the jargon, 'print-dominated media') to another, which was audio-visual. The shift was seen as both technical and qualitative, the new technologies implying new ways of thinking and understanding.

This extension of Marshall McLuhan's dictum that 'the medium is the message' created a sense of vague panic among those educated in the old ideologies by the old print technologies, which was compounded during the 1980s by the erosion of other certainties: the gradual collapse of communism and the triumph of consumerist economic theories in the Western democracies and Japan. Consumption was equated with freedom and the images created by advertising with meaning, as part of a process of deception that ceased to be one because it consciously involved each side in a game: the consumer was no longer the victim of fallacious claims, but a participant in the fallacy, willingly espousing the adman's assertion that the latest trainers, the latest video game, the newest piece of electronic hardware, acquired an instrinsic value because of their novelty. To be seen to be at the leading edge was a good in itself.

The Pompidou Centre in Paris had recognized the importance of the audio-visual media in the 1970s, and they came to play an expanded role in education and museum design during the following decade. There were museums devoted entirely to the visual arts, most of them inaugurated in a spirit of self-criticism rather than self-congratulation, on the assumption that they were long overdue: in Britain, the National Museum of Film, Photography and Television opened in Bradford in 1983 and the Museum of the Moving Image in London in 1988. In France, Senator René Monory, seeking a means to revitalize his relatively impoverished and mainly agricultural *département* of the Vienne, decided to install the European Park of the Image on a site a few miles outside Poitiers. Pointedly named 'Futuroscope', it included research centres, a technical *lycée* and university complex, and a theme park designed to expand constantly so that it could include every example of visual technology: a giant Imax screen, a domed Omnimax cinema (with a fish-eye lens), a 'dynamic' cinema (with moving seats, to simulate, for example, the sensations of a roller-coaster ride), a 3D-cinema, a 360° circular screen, a 'magic carpet' cinema (with images projected under the spectators' feet) and 'Imax Solido' (a three-dimensional image projected through liquid crystal spectacles, opening in 1993).

The heart of Futuroscope is the 'experience'. As anyone who has seen Imax or Omnimax will know, the material that can be shown on these systems is, for the time being, intrinsically rather uninteresting. The Imax camera, for example, is bulky, and only capable of quite short takes before the film has to be changed; the system is also very expensive and the product can only be exhibited on the immense screens designed for the purpose, such as those at Bradford and Poitiers. Like the rest of the new technologies in Futuroscope, it has a limited repertoire of documentaries — scenes from space or underwater (Imax and Omnimax), the Tour de France (on the 360° screen), roller-coasters and skiers (the 'dynamic' cinema), and so on. The technology is the message.

In some ways, this recalls developments in cinema technology during the 1950s, partly in response to the challenge of television: cinemascope, 3D, Todd-AO and so on. The difference is that where new technologies (like 'scope and, later, Dolby sound) could be incorporated into the network for exhibiting films and easily exploited for a range of film narratives, they were adopted; otherwise they were abandoned, like the 1950s experiments with 3D using red and green glasses. In brief, the technology was only seen as useful and valuable if it could offer more than the sensation of novelty, and rapidly become so familiar that spectators no longer noticed it. Audiences in 1955 may have been prepared to forgive the inadequacies of *Underwater!* for the sake of the underwater photography, but their indulgence would not extend beyond the second or third film of that sort.

Futuroscope, on the other hand, is constructed around the premise that audiences will travel a long way to see anything that provides them with a new visual experience. If the systems on display are used to convey no message more important than the sensation of receiving it, is this really because they involve technologies that are still in their infancy? The technologies appear to be ever more fully developed, even if what they have to say is infantile.

This is not entirely irrelevant to the cinema as a whole. The rapid development of new technologies during the 1970s and 1980s was a response to much the same pressures as those that caused the same phenomenon during the 1950s: competition from other media. They aimed to demonstrate how the large screen could offer a different experience from the small one. The world audience for cinema had two broad characteristics; it was predominantly youthful (teenagers and young adults), and it was falling. In France, from an overall figure of 201.9 million in 1982 it dropped to 117 million in 1991. Within this, the fall was even sharper for French films: 107.8 million to 35.2 million, a loss of 67.4 %. For American films, on the other hand, it actually rose over the same ten-year period, from 60.7 million to 68.7 million (up 13.2 %). Of course, the budgets of French producers were usually well below those of Hollywood, but this only served as further evidence that the audience liked big-budget pictures, with star names and impressive special effects.

The answer was to adopt some of Hollywood's appeal, within the limitations of French budgets; and this remains the solution recommended by the Cluzel report of early 1993: to allow the audience to decide what films it wants to see and to make them, rather than creating audiences for the films that are made. This was also, broadly, the response of Hollywood during the period, and explains the number of sequels and 'look-alikes', *Home Alone* being followed by *Home Alone 2: Lost in New York*, or *Honey, I Shrunk the Kids* by *Honey, I Blew Up the Kid*. Note that, as a French answer to the challenge of Hollywood, this solution is the contrary of the 'new technology' one: novelties are supposed to counter competition by offering something different, imitation by offering more of the same. Apart from this, the French answer has been a high level of government subsidy to the industry, and some attempts to control the exhibition of films on television or to find ways of returning television money to cinema producers.

The age group which composed the greater part of the cinema audience had many calls on its money: clothes and other leisure activities, like video games, records, cassettes and the hardware associated with these, including innovations like personal stereos and CD players. New film-makers, among them Beineix, addressed this generation in a 'language' that gave priority over language to sound and vision — the 'language', that is to say, of the pop video, where meanings are not primarily conveyed by narrative and argument; or, rather, where narrative and argument are encapsulated in image, style and sound, and the spectator's emotions are stimulated by these rather than by dialogue. The point about American films is not so much that they represented the American way of life, as that they were, to a young French audience, culturally, linguistically and socially non-specific. The young French man or woman who adopted styles of dress and a few English words from an American movie was not trying to pass as American, but affirming his or her distance from French norms. It was, in many ways, like a process of adolescent self-discovery through experimentation with different personae.

Léos Carax's *Mauvais sang* (1986) and Luc Besson's *Subway* (1985) and *Nikita* (1990) mirror this precisely. *Mauvais sang* is a science-fiction thriller about the theft of a serum which will cure a disease much like AIDS which afflicts those who make love without love. Alex (the remarkable-looking Denis Lavant) is a young street entertainer and cardsharp, the sort of person who hangs around outside the Pompidou Centre on a warm afternoon, drawn into the intrigue partly because his late father was somehow involved, and partly through love of Juliette Binoche. The love story is touching, the style is resolutely modern, sexually explicit and energetic, but the thriller narrative is virtually incomprehensible. Two veterans of the genre, Michel Piccoli and Serge Reggiani, make appearances, almost as icons of an earlier cinema age.

Subway opens with a heart-stopping car chase that ends with Christophe Lambert driving directly down the steps of an entrance to the Paris métro. Besson at first wanted Sting for the part, but Lambert (half-American, at least) was a more than adequate substitute. He plays a safecracker, escaping with some documents stolen from a crooked businessman who is married to his girlfriend (Isabelle Adjani); he decides to hide out among the *marginaux* (petty thieves, drop-outs, misfits) who supposedly live in the service areas behind the métro. Like so many other heroes on the run, he is pursued both by the Mob and by the police.

Despite its title, *Subway* is entirely 'French' in setting, language and atmosphere. The sets were even designed by the veteran Alexandre Trauner, who did the art direction for René Clair's *Sous les toits de Paris* (1930) — the first major French talking picture — as well as for the Marcel Carné-Jacques Prévert films of the 1930s; so much for youth culture. One of the central scenes in the picture shows Adjani rebelling against the stuffiness of a typical bourgeois dinner, before opting to join Lambert. Otherwise, there is very little plot, the message being in the excitement and the display of alternative lifestyles. You can be French, Besson says, without being like your parents.

Nikita picks up the theme. The central character here is a young woman (Anne Parillaud), who is arrested and sentenced to life imprisonment for killing three policemen during an armed robbery. The robbery, which opens the film, corresponds to the excitement of the opening car chase in *Subway*, but is far more violent. Nikita herself is brutal and aggressive, while Fred (Lambert) was efficient and composed: a complete social misfit, she kills without compunction and is subject to uncontrollable rages against authority. Her favourite expletive is '*enculé(s)*!', which the dictionary classifies as one of those expressions that are 'liable to offend in any situation': Nikita certainly wishes to cause the greatest possible offence. We are not expected either to admire or condemn this character, but to identify with her, as totally unbourgeois and as a rebel against all convention; almost as a force of nature.

Once again, Besson takes a stereotypical situation from the genre and imagines that an undercover agency of the government, realizing Nikita's potential, has decided to employ her. She is drugged and reduced, temporarily, to a weeping baby, calling for her mother. She is then told that she has been reported dead (suicide in prison) and that she has no alternative but to cooperate. She is trained in the use of weapons, in martial arts and (by Jeanne Moreau) in how to pass as a woman — a skill that she had not learned in her previous, tomboy-with-a-tommy-gun incarnation. Having started as an urban savage, she is now a sort of urban Cinderella, ready to be launched on a career of assassination on behalf of her masters. Improbably, she falls in love with the checkout boy at the supermarket and ends as a vulnerable young woman, crying: 'I can't go on!'

This second rebirth looks suspiciously like an attempt to have it both ways, expecting us at first to sympathize with Nikita's uncompromising pursuit of freedom and her refusal to conform to any of the stereotypes of 'feminine' behaviour, then to believe that she is, after all, capable of finer feelings. In the end, like *Subway*, *Nikita* is not about character, but about violence, energy, dynamism and, most of all, about cinematic style. In common with many films of its kind during the 1980s, it was routinely, and slightly dismissively, compared with pop video; and there is some truth in the analogy. From the opening frames, Besson is concerned with creating a visual style, mainly through the use of colour, in order to direct and concentrate the audience's attention, much as the maker of a pop video tries to find a visual language that will not only translate the emotions of the music, but also correspond to the singer or group's significance for its fans: cool, folksy, jazzy, heavy metal, futuristic, nostalgic, political, ecological . . . The pop video is a means of selling music and, like a television commercial, sets out to establish a distinctive brand image through the use of visual clues. *Nikita* has a brand image — cold colours (particularly blues), artificial light, hard edges: the feel of gunmetal. The world of the film is functional and impersonal, and the style alluring so that, instead of directing our attention to the human significance of the action, it distances us, and invites us to take pleasure in its cool efficiency. From *Diva* and *Subway* to *Nikita*, the post-modern thriller was sharpening the surface image for its own sake, like a hyper-realist painting, without much concern with what was represented or belief in its 'meaning'. '*C'est du cinoche*,' a character in *Nikita* remarks — 'it's cinema', or, as translated in the English subtitle: 'It's just for show'.

Some of the major figures in French cinema continued to work, however, and to believe that meaning could still be inherent in character and narrative. Chabrol's 'Inspector Lavardin' series (*Poulet au vinaigre*, 1984 — neatly retitled *Cop au vin* for English-speaking audiences, and *Inspecteur Lavardin*, 1986), with Jean Poiret as a middle-aged detective, were traditional investigative stories exploring the underside of bourgeois life in provincial France (a sub-genre that dates back to Simenon). Claude Zidi's *Les Ripoux* (1985) and its sequel are entertaining comedies, based on the premise that there are two kinds of corruption: the amiable variety practised by Philippe Noiret, a veteran of the Paris force who happily accepts bribes and turns a blind eye to minor misdemeanours, while looking forward to a pleasant retirement betting on the *tiercé*; and the more vicious corruption of the young thugs who are brought in to replace him, but cannot distinguish between taking a small pay-off from petty criminals and putting them out of business by bleeding them dry.

The films are funny, but soft-centered, taking the old theme of police complicity with criminals and turning it into a lesson for life. When Noiret is given a priggish and ambitious young partner (Thierry Lhermitte), it takes time to re-educate the new boy in the wisdom of custom. Around the improbable father-son relationship between the characters played by Noiret and Lhermitte, Zidi develops the themes of comradeship, compassion and tolerance that have been central to the tradition of French film comedy since Clair and Pagnol.

These are not, however, themes peculiar to the thriller, *film noir, polar, film policier,* gangster film — or whatever term one wishes to use for the genre which is the subject of this book. Is it possible to suggest a definition? I have been working on the premise that there are certain central and abiding preoccupations in this kind of cinema — though, when you try to define them, the result is likely to sound as perverse as a serious-minded attempt at a definition of comedy. Thrillers are entertainment, but no one is likely to be entertained by a definition of their qualities.

Since they deal with crime, they are concerned with matters of legality and illegality, and hence with right and wrong. In so far as the nineteenth-century origins of the genre lie in the detective story, this is incidental, because taken for granted: the narrative is preoccupied with identification of the perpetrator. But the antecedents are mixed: gothic novels, horror stories and what were known in England as 'penny dreadfuls', also contributed to a genre that owed something to the sense of anonymity felt by inhabitants of large cities, and the menace felt by property-owners at the growth of an urban underclass. In America, the lawlessness of the Prohibition era helped to create a class of cinema films, the gangster movie, which was characterized by a distinctive aesthetic style. Out of it grew the American *films noirs* of the 1940s expressing a sense of fatalism through dark tones, menacing shadows, disturbing camera angles and narrative devices that included flashbacks, voice-overs and ironic plotlines in which the characters merely seemed to be active participants in their own stories, their destinies in fact being decided by the workings of an impersonal fate.

The neat cause-and-effect reasoning of the English detective story was challenged by a New World in which accident, rather than reason, decided the fate of the protagonists; and, in France, by a 'poetic realism' that came to similar conclusions about the human place in the universe. Yet if human beings were victims of fate, how far could they be considered guilty of their misdeeds? The murderer who is trapped by chance rather than by the skill of the police or the private detective, is going to appear himself a victim of bad luck — all the more so if we have been encouraged to admire his ingenuity in concealing his crime.

Our admiration for the cleverness and energy of the wrongdoers is bound to be ambivalent: for the most part, we are on the side of the law. Therefore, if legality is central, so too is evil, and the problem of evil, and the ambivalence of our responses to it. In protestant America, the motivation for crime is most often sex or greed, the latter an impulse that is legitimate when it serves the needs of the capitalist state, illegitimate when it ignores them and tries to circumvent the system; the distinction between the methods of acquiring wealth, powered as they are by the same impulse, becomes a central problem in films, from the 1930s and 1940s gangster movies to *The Godfather* (where the difference between big business and crime is virtually abolished). The characters belong either to a criminal underworld, distinct from 'normal' society, or else to a small range of almost equally marginal professions: actresses and singers, journalists, private eyes, insurance salesmen . . . The pessimism of American *film noir* is frequently conveyed through the theme of corruption (of politicians and police), adding a social dimension to the malignity of the universe.

In catholic and republican France, the motivations for evil

are usually more obscure. Sex is less threatening, and so creates fewer of those sinister undercurrents that fuel the Hollywood films of uncontrollable passion. The characters, even in an urban setting, are more precisely situated in their social roles and geographical location. The ambiguity, in the post-war world, comes from a deeper mistrust of the authorities which is not to do with illegitimacy (corruption), but with a more fundamental questioning of the legitimacy of all authority and of the state itself. The experience of the Occupation also suggests themes of betrayal and treachery, suspicion of one's neighbours, who may be the school mistress of *Les Diaboliques* or the butcher of *Le Boucher*; and a sense of the unknowability of the Other.

During the 1950s, as we have seen, 'continental' films like *Les Diaboliques* were often met in Anglo-Saxon countries with the charge of 'immorality', because of their frankness about sex or because of their sympathy in the depiction of wrong-doers, or because they rejected the conventional endings which attempt to prove that crime is always rewarded by punishment. Similar charges might be levelled against *Le Boucher*, which depicts a compulsive murderer with sympathy and implies that human beings are natural savages, who have only recently been decked out in 'civilized' codes of behaviour. Or to the political thrillers of the 1970s, which question the legitimacy of the political state.

With hindsight, these charges can been seen to be misguided. These films may have rejected conventional narrative formulae (crime leading to punishment, criminals clearly identified by their unpleasant appearance and behaviour), but they were still centrally concerned with questions of morality. Incidentally, the extreme reaction of some critics in Britain during the 1950s provides a useful benchmark, because British society at that time displayed peculiarly conformist attitudes towards the state as a guardian of public morals — so that it was possible, for example, for a clergyman to write to the *Radio Times* complaining of a radio play that ended with an innocent man going to the gallows as immoral, because it dared to suggest that such a miscarriage of justice was conceivable in the British legal system. Public opinion in Britain was to be changed, painfully, by a succession of wrong or questionable verdicts (Timothy Evans, Ruth Ellis, Derek Bentley), while in France this kind of demonstration would cause less of a stir: the events of the Occupation and the *épuration* had already provided enough proof of the fallibility of the state and its justice.

Where the charge does begin to stick, is at the point when the genre begins to relinquish altogether its preoccupation with matters of right and wrong, goodness and evil. To interpret the language of the thriller and *film noir* as purely an aesthetic code — to study the grammar and structures as a system of signs only, losing faith or losing interest in their potential as referents — is to abandon the essential.

Film noir developed a distinctive aesthetic: lighting, camera angles, narrative devices, designed to convey excitement, suspense, a sense of unease and menace, fatalism and paranoia. The purpose of this was not primarily aesthetic; it grew out of a desire to tell stories that addressed questions which were ultimately philosophical or moral, to do with the nature of crime, personality, social relations or the workings of fate. This purpose is lost in films that merely reproduce the aesthetic, and the loss is crucial.

This is why the brilliance and invention of films like *Détective* and *Nikita* is ultimately unsatisfying: the individual elements of the genre appear to be present, assembled with considerable skill, but the purpose has vanished. Its disappearance is not at first obvious: the early films of Godard, for example, amount to a comment on the influence of American cinema in France, and it is possible to interpret a number of French examples of the genre as being partly concerned with this. But, by the time we reach *Subway* and *Nikita*, the empty space can no longer be concealed. Here are films that use the language of the thriller without the underlying moral and philosophical intentions of the thriller, just as they use the aesthetic of the television commercial to sell nothing except themselves.

It was not only in France that this happened; it seemed that a succession of film-makers was setting out to produce work that had no other purpose except to attract the label *'film noir'*. What was disappointing about these efforts was not even their self-consciousness, but a vacuity that betrayed an essentially trivialising attitude to everything that is most important in human existence. The relaxation of constraints on the depiction of sex and violence, which had made it possible for cinema to deal with them directly, also opened the way for films in which sexual acts and killings became routine and meaningless. What had been a source of anxiety in early *film noir*, because it had to be described circumspectly in order to placate the censor, ceased to arouse any anxiety at all, because it was just *du cinoche*: the killings were only pretend, however bloody, the sex was a selling point for an audience mainly composed of teenagers and young adults who wanted it to be uncomplicated, in fiction at least, like a holiday from the disturbing emotions of real life. To appeal to the same audience, directors like Carax and Beineix added a touch of designer romanticism: the virus in *Mauvais sang* afflicts those who cannot love, the killing machine in *Nikita* is a little girl at heart.

Not everyone, thankfully, followed the trend.

VII.

BACK TO BASE

Robert Bresson was 75 when he made *L'Argent* (1982), a late masterpiece in an altogether exemplary career. He is always treated as an outsider among directors, individual in both style and subject-matter. Yet, as we have seen, his work has served as a model and an inspiration to others: his first major international success, *Un condamné à mort s'est échappé* (1956), though not a crime story, is one of the great suspense films and arguably a great *film noir*. His religious concerns might seem irrelevant to a genre that is usually characterized by a cynical outlook on humankind and a preoccupation with violence and sex. Bresson's religion (rather different from the legacy of Hitchcock's catholic childhood), belongs to the austere, Jansenist strain of French catholicism, with its emphasis on divine grace and predestination — a powerful influence on French catholic writers, in part because of its assocation with the great figures of seventeenth-century literature, Jean Racine and Blaise Pascal. This odd combination of catholic ritual with almost Calvinist beliefs can be felt to some extent in the work of France's major twentieth-century catholic writers: Paul Claudel, François Mauriac and Georges Bernanos (whose novel, *Journal d'un curé de campagne*, was the source for Bresson's fourth film, made in 1950). It is an uncomfortable doctrine, which sees life as a drama of suffering, renunciation and the search for purity in a universe blighted by original sin, and governed by a remote and impersonal divine will.

L'Argent opens with a schoolboy asking his middle-class parents for more pocket money. Hardly anything is said; but the father's refusal to look up from his desk and the mother's concern with getting out of the house tell us a great deal about the coldness and lack of affection in the relationship between parents and child. This failure of communication, which is also a failure of parental care, will be the first cause of Bresson's tragedy: the boy is tempted by a schoolfriend to pass a forged note, and they succeed in doing so because their middle-class background makes them look honest. The note, and the blame, pass from one hand to another, with consequences that spread and gather force exponentially as the trail leads towards prison, murder and finally a measure of redemption: 'oh, money, visible god, what would you not lead us to do?'

For the greater part of the film, all exchanges are reduced to the pattern of financial transactions, even when actual financial transactions are not involved. The protagonists communicate across desks, counters, tables, the judge's bench in the court, the glass panel in a prison visiting room. Instead of showing us greed in terms of the characters' dreams of what money can buy, Bresson actualizes the desire for money and its effects in concrete terms, as a barrier to human contact, promoting deceit and corrupting relationships. The motive of greed and the mechanics of fate, prime causes in the plot of so many crime stories, are here exposed with relentless logic. What emerges most clearly from the demonstration is that the austere Jansenist has a standpoint that allows him to bring out what is crucial to the narrative:

not violence, action or style, but a sense of sin.

This is not to say that one needs to be a French catholic to make crime thrillers. What is essential, however, is a concern with morality, with the world as, in some sense or other, a battleground between notions of right and wrong. This does not mean a simple division of characters into 'goodies' and 'baddies', or even an explicit confrontation between the two sides: many of the characters in *film noir* are morally ambiguous and the purpose is often to demonstrate that the line dividing, say, police from criminals or hunter from hunted, is morally almost invisible. The vision may be so bleak as to suggest goodness and rightness only by their absence, or to present them as the illusions of a corrupt and sinful world. But in all these cases a central concern is to assert, assess, explore, confront, analyze or challenge moral values, and the aesthetics of the work derive from that, not the other way about. The attention and participation of the audience is engaged by this conflict, not by style or technique.

Eric Rochant's otherwise rather slight film, *Au yeux du monde* (1991), reads like an example of Monsieur Bresson's good influence: a young man (Yvan Attal) hijacks a school bus in a futile attempt to prove himself to his girlfriend. In the course of their journey around the countryside, he wins the sympathy of the pupils and of their teacher (Kristin Scott-Thomas), while himself undergoing a sort of conversion as he comes to understand his own loneliness and inadequacies. Clearly not a criminal type, he is still capable of committing a crime and terrorising innocent people; yet the truth is that he is also a product of circumstances. By the end, the two sides, criminal and victims, have drawn closer together, and learned how to deal with one another with affection rather than aggression.

The moral ambiguity of police work, from being one of the genre's discoveries has almost become one of its clichés; it is, at the very least, taken for granted. Maurice Pialat's *Police* (1985) makes the assertion through the familiar storyline of the cop who falls in love with a woman from the wrong side of the law. Gérard Depardieu plays Mangin, a plainclothes policeman in the immigrant quarter of Belleville — the similarity between Mangin's colleagues and the drug dealers whom they hunt is underlined by the fact all wear the same uniform of black leather jackets and speak the same language, a dialect compounded of the slang common among all French teenagers: *se fringer*, 'to dress up', for example, or *le poignon*, ('money'), with an assortment of slightly more professional terms: *de la poudre* ('heroin'), *des flingues* ('guns'), and so on. Nothing to bother the average audience, nothing as inventive as the language of *Série noire*.

Between Mangin and the drug dealers, the law and the law-breakers, is a defence lawyer, Lambert (Richard Anconina), who acknowledges that his clients are 'all guilty'. Mangin's friendly relationship with this go-between is as significant as his habit of roughing up suspects, and as suspicious as the luxury of his apartment (which he admits is a sign of corruption). The absence of music on the sound-track, the darkness of the screen (much of the action takes place at night, in the streets or in ill-lit interiors) and the photography (characters in close-up or medium close-up) convey a feeling of claustrophobia. Mangin is trapped in this tiny quarter of Paris, where sex, money and drugs are the motors for an inescapable cycle of corruption and hopelessness.

The difference between Mangin and the rest is that he is more alive to his situation and aware, in particular, of the impossibility of normal relationships, of love and affection, in this stifling climate. '*Vous êtes complètement cinglé, Mangin* (you're nuts),' one of his colleagues tells him; but we sense that his violent behaviour is a reponse to an inner despair, and that there is truth in his self-mockery when he says: 'My mother didn't love me, so I take it out on all women,' or 'I've never loved anyone.'

Needless to say, he does fall in love, with Noria (Sophie Marceau), the mistress of a North African belonging to the drug ring that Mangin is trying to break up. But is love possible in this poisoned society? Mangin discovers that Noria is unknowable, not only a habitual liar, but perhaps a non-person, a shifting identity which takes on the colour of its surroundings and may be as incapable of love as Mangin claims to be himself. 'She fucks whoever she likes, she lies as easily as she breathes,' Lambert tells him. Even her name, 'Noria', is false, adopted to identify with the Arabs whose culture, alien and impenetrable, she presents as the only authentic reality in the world of the film. In the end, for the sake of Noria, Mangin is drawn irrevocably into complicity with the underworld, his attempt to redeem himself through love having succeeded only in closing his one remaining avenue of escape.

The film was a success, but attracted criticism for its treatment of racial issues and of women. These are both sensitive areas. Pialat's North Africans are less stereotyped than some of those in Bob Swaim's *La Balance* (1982), and it is true that crime, especially drug-dealing, exists in areas like Belleville; and there is undoubtedly racism among members of the Paris police force. But, given the hostility felt by some people to North African immigrants and the way this has been exploited during the 1980s by the National Front, even Noria's assertion that the Arabs 'have their own reality' might be taken as discriminatory. In fact Noria, the French character in the film who has most sympathy for the Arabs, may not be the best spokesperson for them.

Much the same applies to the treatment of women: the case for the defence would be that Pialat exposes some realities in police attitudes and that his central female character is determined by the plot. It didn't help that relations between the director and the female lead were poor, and that Sophie Marceau accused him of having treated her like 'a sado-masochistic pervert' during the making of the film. However, aside from these off-screen exchanges, one can see *Police* as the investigation of failures in understanding between individuals and cultures, as well as unnatural complicities between them, and the impossibility of normal relationships against such a background. Pialat dissects his small corner of Paris to give a grim picture of life inside it; with, at the film's centre, a character whose aspirations suggest at least the possibility of something better outside.

Dédé, the central male figure in *La Balance*, inhabits the same world and shares the same aspirations, though from the other side of the law. Played by Philippe Léotard, whose battered features perfectly suggest a blend of outward mistrust and inner torment, Dédé is a petty criminal whom the police of the Brigades Territoriales plan to use in an elaborate plot to undermine a gang leader (Maurice Ronet, in his last film). In order to persuade Dédé to give evidence, they bring pressure on him firstly by brutality, then (when that fails) by exploiting his love for a prostitute, Nicole (Nathalie Baye).

The morality of the film is not orthodox, but conventional for the genre: the criminal 'godfathers' are corrupt, but so are the police, who have no scruples in the methods they use: one suspects that, like all those who believe that the ends justify the means, they have become so inured to deceit and violence that they have long since forgotten the ultimate purpose these are supposed to serve. Dédé and Nicole, on the other hand, though they have little respect for the law, stick firmly to their principles. They are loyal to each other and to the code that despises the informer (*'la balance'*) — the individual who has no code, and appears to be on one side while working for the other. The informer's crime in not only deceit, but lack of integrity and authenticity, qualities which Dédé possesses in abundance: when the police set out to divide his loyalties (to Nicole and to the underworld code), the audience is drawn into his inner conflict.

However, this central theme is only introduced after a prologue in which we are asked to identify with the police (led by Richard Berry), and one of their informers, who is murdered at the start of the film. The moral focus thus shifts, suggesting that we question our instinctive sympathy with the forces of law and order, and consider whether Dédé's code may not represent a higher morality, more altruistic because it is based on respect for others, and more principled because it defines the limits of behaviour within which Dédé can respect himself. Dédé's values are intrinsic, while those of the police are extrinsic: the uniform and the legal code that it represents legitimize their behaviour, relieving them of responsibility for their actions. They can cheat, bully, assault, deceive, even kill, in the name of the law. We may approve of their struggle against crime, but when they are ready to use Dédé and Nicole in order to get to Massina (Ronet), we start to perceive them as we might soldiers who would excuse any action on the grounds that they were merely obeying orders.

La Balance follow a pattern established since the Carné-Prévert films of the 1930s, with conventional underworld characters (sympathetic crook, affectionate prostitute) caught up in a story of doomed love. But it is also about individual moral responsibilies, a theme which has acquired a particular resonance since the Second World War. In the last resort, those who are prepared to abrogate their responsibilities in specific cases and use bad means to achieve the ends that others have set them, may well find that the ends themselves are bad (for example, in Vietnam). And, if this seems to overstretch the significance of a 100-minute crime thriller, one can only say that it is more improbable to suppose that genre films will not reflect something of the morality of their time. The simple goodies-and-baddies, cops-and-robbers movies seem trite, not so much because the plots are predictable, but because we no longer possess the moral certainties that they reflected.

Bertrand Tavernier's controversial police procedural, *L.627* (1992), adopts a quite different, almost documentary approach to the work of the drugs squad. Using some professional but little-known actors (Didier Bezace, Charlotte Kady, Philippe Torreton and his son, Nils Tavernier), Tavernier follows the day-to-day activities of the police: questioning suspects, dealing with superiors, meeting informers, staking out or busting into premises, and creates an extraordinarily convincing picture of their work. The absence of any strong storyline actually contibutes to this, but the plausibility of the settings and the language of the group are what chiefly persuade us of the film's authenticity. Tavernier owed much of his information to Michel Alexandre, his co-author on the screenplay and the police officer on whom the main character in the film was loosely based. The director's diary of his year, including the filming and release of *L.627*, was published in *Projections 2* by Faber (1993).

The title refers to the number in the criminal code of the law against dealing in narcotics. This piece of legislation, imposed from somewhere else (that is, by politicians in Parliament), is the one that the officers have to administer in the quite different social reality of the streets: 'logic is logic, rules are rules'. The central figure in the story is 'Lulu' (Didier Bezace), a young cop, dedicated to his work, determined to wipe out what he perceives as an evil, but increasingly aware that he and his colleagues are being denied the proper means to do it. They are like soldiers launched into enemy territory, with a plan of action worked out at a headquarters which remains in sporadic contact with them, but cares very little about their fate. Moreover, the motivations of the group-members vary and there are good and bad among them: racists and thugs, as well as essentially well-meaning officers like 'Lulu'.

Since there is no conventional plot, only a loose storyline that revolves around 'Lulu's' search for the woman who is one of his informers, the progress of the film is spiritual: the progress of its central character towards a more subtle understanding of the issues involved in his work. By the end of the film, 'Lulu' has matured slightly and knows a little more than he did at the start. The advance is small, but real, the lines between good and bad interpretation of the law by its enforcers is a thin one, though no less real for that. The distinctions the film makes may seem slight, though in reality they are crucial (the difference, as Tavernier points out in *Projections*, between the cop who can distinguish an African from Mali and one from Benin, and the cop for whom all black people are just 'Africans'). Of course, the police do take on some of the characteristics of the milieu in which they work, but the film does not succumb to the cynical argument that this puts 'cops' and 'robbers' morally on the same plane. The photography (by Alain Choquart), editing and music (by Philippe Sarde) are superbly exciting, but neither does the film succumb to the temptation to make an aesthetically satisfying and morally neutral film about the nightmare of urban life. The same anger that drives 'Lulu', drives the director.

There is an unending human fascination with the nature of evil, which is to do partly with our sense of the ultimate unknowability of the Other, and partly too with the connection between the nature of evil and the nature of power. *Film noir* is a way of exploring this fascination, which is characterized by the particular aesthetic suggested in the double meaning (literal and figurative) of '*noir*'.

Many of the conditions that produced the classic American *films noirs*, or their French counterparts, no longer apply. Urban life has changed, politics has changed, crime has changed, cinema techniques have changed. Most of all, genres change because film-makers and audiences cannot accept the same story told over and over in the same way. Every film is an assertion which tacitly demands either a counter-assertion, or a refinement, or a development of some sort; there is little point in re-asserting the same thing twice or three times.

However, there may be re-assessments; and, as the 1990s began, French cinema was re-assessing the heritage of the past, particularly those 'well-made' *films noirs* of thirty or forty years earlier, to see what they had to say about the nature of evil in our own time. In *Monsieur Hire* (1990) Patrice Leconte remade a Simenon story that had been filmed in 1948 by Julien Duvivier, as *Panique*. In the same year, Christian de Chalonge dramatized the historical crimes of *Docteur Petiot*. To these films, with obvious links to the era of 1940s *film noir*, I should like to add another, in which there is no such evident connection: the Franco-Dutch co-production, directed by George Sluizer, *The Vanishing* (1988).

Monsieur Hire is the story of a voyeur, beautifully shot, against a neo-baroque score by Michael Nyman. From his room in a typical French apartment block, the lonely Hire (Michel Blanc) watches Alice (Sandrine Bonnaire) on the other side of the central courtyard as she dresses and undresses, or makes love with her boyfriend (Luc Thuillier). When a young child is murdered in the neighbourhood, suspicion naturally falls on Hire — our suspicion and that of the police. Meanwhile, Hire has shyly made contact with Alice, and we follow the progress of a repressed, middle-aged man's unrealizable dream of love for this young woman.

Any film that has a voyeur as its central character is saying something about the camera-eye, the intrusions of the film-maker and the desires of the audience. In Michael Powell's *Peeping Tom* (1960), the statement read like a confession; in *Monsieur Hire*, like an apology. Appearances can be deceptive, and it is love and loneliness, not guilt, that destroy Hire. The impulse of the voyeur, here, is not to assert power, but to reach out towards a world of human warmth and sexual pleasure from which he has been excluded by his circumstances and personality.

In both films, the nature of the central character and the motives for his action only emerge piecemeal, and our attitudes towards them change correspondingly. The camera may act as the eyes of a voyeur, but the motive can be understanding, as well as power, perhaps leading to sympathy with the underdog as well as admiration for the energy of the Devil. But it is the more exciting game of getting close to the Devil that provides the basic material for the thriller.

What kind of a man was Dr. Petiot? The reality was not quite what we see in the film: the historical doctor had already shown signs of psychological disturbance and criminal tendencies even before he embarked on his career of mass murder. What Christian de Chalonge does, admirably helped by Michel Serrault in the leading part, is to explore the inner life of a man from whose personality something is missing: clearly, an ability to sympathize with others, but also a real sense of his own identity. This Petiot is an actor, unable to throw off his part because he has no authentic self to return to. He can charm and he can heal, he can deceive and he can kill, simply because he has learned the roles to perfection.

The film analyzes the character of this psychopath (who, in the event, went to the guillotine with a joke to the priest, apparently untroubled by the prospect of his own death); and also exploits the aesthetic heritage of German Expressionism: the outer world of Paris during the Occupation, the blackout, the drab streets, long passageways and dark tunnels, reflect Petiot's inner darkness. There is a similar image at the start of *The Vanishing*, though here it represents the fears of the victim, or the search for enlightenment that is a guiding theme of the film. The dark tunnel, opening into sunlight, that features at the start (and the 'golden egg' in the girl's dream, which is the title of Tim Krabbé's original novel) might also derive from accounts of near-death experiences in which patients have recorded out-of-body sensations and visions of journeys through darkness towards light.

The Vanishing was remade in the United States in 1993, with significant changes to suit an American audience. The original version is a haunting and powerful film. A young Dutch couple (Gene Bervoets and Johanna Ter Steege) are on holiday in the South of France and stop at a petrol station. The young woman goes to buy some soft drinks in the shop and disappears. For years afterwards, Rex is obsessed with trying to find out whether she is alive or dead, and what happened to her, partly because of his promise, just before she vanished, that he would never abandon her, but chiefly because of the intellectual torment created by this vacuum in his life. The audience, meanwhile, learns who is responsible, though it has to share the young man's uncertainty about the precise circumstances of the girl's death until the end of the film.

The killer, Raymond (Bernard-Pierre Donnadieu), finally contacts Rex and offers to satisfy his curiosity. Raymond is an apparently happily married man, with two daughters, dissatisfied with his job as a chemistry teacher, but otherwise leading an average, even boring life. He does reveal a liking for slightly cruel practical jokes, but there is nothing unusual about that. He is even capable of heroism and altruism: we learn that he has saved a young child from drowning.

As a result of that action, his younger daughter comes to regard him as a hero, and this makes him wonder whether he is also capable of great evil. An incident in childhood has suggested to him that the only way to achieve freedom and self-knowledge is to test oneself to the limit of one's imagination. He begins meticulously to plan the foulest act that he can think of, a gratuitous crime committed for the same motives as the *acte gratuit* in André Gide's *Les Faux-monnayeurs*.

Evil as power; the banality of evil. Like Petiot, Raymond is that most reassuring of figures, a member of the professional middle-class. He fascinates us as he fascinates Rex, because we want to know what lies beneath the surface of the reality around us. We want to look into the mind of the killer, see how he resembles us and what he is capable of doing. Safe on our side of the screen, we can share his fears and his excitement, without having to take responsibility for what he does. The audience, too, has its motives.

The undeniable motive, however, is to be entertained. From

the second and third decades of this century onwards, Hollywood created the world's most powerful medium for entertainment, against which others are judged and with which they must inevitably compete. The outcome is a dialogue between American and other cinema industries, in which they adopt or reject its codes and it either ignores what they are doing, or remoulds their product to suit its conventions: the case of *The Vanishing* is characteristic — a Franco-Dutch film, remade by the original director with whatever modifications are necessary for it to be saleable on the American market.

The history of the thriller has been typical of this history of exchange. Hollywood films offered excitements that the audience craved, but translating them to European settings involved changes, not least at the level of language. Other elements (police procedure, criminal methods, social backgrounds, characters) had to be modified before they became plausible in a different context. The process involved criticism and analysis, and new perceptions that could be transferred back to source.

The thriller has its origins in the epic mode of melodrama, where the struggle between God and Satan is transposed to the everyday context of life in the modern city, the nineteenth-century city with its mobs and slums. Out of this urban jungle come the individual figures of the criminal and the policeman, each from the start potentially 'corrupted' by the fact that they inhabit the same environment, the policeman tempted to adopt the wrongdoer's methods to achieve his ends, the criminal having to wear a disguise of respectability to cover his crimes, and possibly slipping into the role of *justicier* or lone vigilante (*Judex*). He has, in any case, his own code of morality.

The policeman's work is not punishment, but identification. The intellectual game in which he engages is diverting in itself and gives rise to the investigative crime story. The skill of the lone detective is to solve puzzles that baffle the regular forces of the police, so Holmes only bothers with the most difficult cases, usually those where the criminal has been particularly ingenious in concealing his crime. The result is the cliché of the least likely suspect, which remains an intellectual game so long as all the suspects are eccentrics (*L'Assassin habite au 21*) but has other implications when they are 'ordinary' people (*Le Corbeau*): the intellectual diversion is revitalized by social criticism and by the implication that any one of us may have criminal tendencies. The focus shifts back to the psychology of the criminal and the morality of individual acts.

However, not all crimes are individual crimes and not all policemen operate as lone detectives. The American gangster movies of the 1930s explored a specifically American reality, but offered a universal model. The organized criminal belonged to an alternative society, with ambitions and codes of behaviour that were, in a sense, a perversion of the accepted social norms. The aspirations of gangsters were little different from those of most other people in capitalist societies: to make money, enjoy the good life, exercise power, gain the respect of their fellow men and eventually retire to a place in the country. Their 'work' demanded qualities, such as courage, nerve and determination, which were the same as those of more honourable professions, like soldiering; the repression of crime was seen as a war, so there might be good and bad on either side (*Touchez pas au grisbi*). The criminal's work also demanded skills, which were in themselves admirable, aside from their ends; and any craftsman is interesting to watch (*Du rififi chez les hommes*).

The period following the Second World War, particularly in Europe, saw a re-evaluation, not least of the 'ordinary' human potential for evil. The war itself had been ambiguous in other respects in the countries occupied by the Nazis: in the battle between the (legal) authorities and the (illegal) Resistance, goodies and baddies changed sides. What was defined as 'crime' might represent a revolt against an oppressive or illegitimate authority. Moreover, the criminal 'heroes' of American movies had an energy and a style that was undeniably attractive. Godard acknowledged it in *A bout de souffle* and *Pierrot le fou*. Satan has often had the best songs.

For a long time, the narrative code of the genre meant that criminals had to be punished in the last reel, either by identification and arrest, or by death. This inevitable fate of the criminal 'heroes' made them also victims: in reality, victims of a narrative convention, they appeared as victims of impersonal forces, tragic as well as criminal heroes. Like those other conventions of plot (the least likely suspect, policeman as criminal, transfer of guilt), this one could have effects that subverted its original implications. But conventions, like the genres that are constructed out of them, become tired — and so open to question. By the late 1980s, audiences were hardly likely to notice — and not to object — that the murderers in *Monsieur Hire* and *The Vanishing* are allowed to get away with their crimes, and the innocent protagonists in both films are the ones who die.

The police, from being the heroes, became the villains and are once more in the process of rehabilitation — not as heroes, perhaps, but acknowledged as being on the right side in the war (*L. 627*). The character of the urban jungle has changed: the victims of drug addiction may be our children; the crime on the streets of the city is no longer a mystery, taking place in an underworld disguised behind a façade of normality, but the outcome of poverty and deprivations that are visible, located in particular districts which threaten to overflow and engulf the rest. The front line is not in the back rooms of the bars in Montmartre, but openly displayed on the streets of Belleville.

Among their other concerns, *film noir* and its associated or derivitive genres have addressed such fears. The trouble with the genre label is that it has to be applied retrospectively: the film-maker who sets out to make 'a *film noir*' is like the Christian who has ambitions to be a saint — in danger of missing the point. The revival of *film noir*, particularly the Hollywood examples of the past decade (I am thinking of films like Kenneth Branagh's *Dead Again*), will insist on illustrating the fact. Perhaps there is no genuine *film noir* outside the Hollywood of the 1940s and early 1950s, when a particular style of film-making happened to suit the concerns of the time.

The questions that preoccupied French directors and audiences were inevitably rather different. What I have tried to do in this book is to identify those concerns, to show how they have been explored through the narratives of the crime movie and to suggest some of the varied social, historical and fictional sources on which they drew. Unlike the pure genre of *film noir*, that story continues, because the issues that such films address — issues of justice, morality and legality — are always open, whether or not the crime is solved and the villain dies in the last reel.

FILMOGRAPHY

ONE HUNDRED AND ONE FRENCH FILMS NOIRS

The listing aims to be inclusive rather than exclusive: in other words, it does not try to define the genres (thriller, *polar*, suspense movie, crime movie, courtroom movie or *film noir*), but to suggest the variety of works that have been made within these categories. The films cover 52 years, from 1942 to 1993.

Titles are listed in alphabetical order [with the English title for release in Britain or the USA in square brackets], ignoring the French definite article (*le, la, l', les*), but not the indefinite article, *Un* or *Une* (i.e. *La Vérité sur Bébé Donge* appears at 'V'; *Une si jolie petite plage* at 'U'). Titles are followed by the date of production, the indication 'bw' if the film was made in black-and-white and the running time. Filmographies are listed using the following abbreviations:

d.: director

sc.: scriptwriter(s)

ph.: photographer

m.: music

ad.: art direction

p.: producer/production company

with: leading players

A BOUT DE SOUFFLE
[BREATHLESS]

1960. bw. 90 mins.
d. Jean-Luc Godard
sc. Godard
ph. Raoul Coutard
m. Martial Solal
p. SNC
with: Jean-Paul Belmondo, Jean Seberg, Jean-Pierre Melville,
Daniel Boulanger

A young tear-away (Belmondo) steals a car, kills a policeman and goes on the run across Paris with an American girl
(Seberg). Godard's first feature is a classic of the New Wave,
dedicated to the American studio Monogram Pictures and
offering a collage of audio and visual styles (Mozart, jazz;
jump cuts, hand-held camera) which enchanted most critics
in France and abroad, though some were disturbed by
Godard's refusal to judge his characters and by the frank
treatment of their sexual relationship. 'The young French
directors,' Pauline Kael wrote, 'discovered the poetry of
crime in American life (from our movies) and showed the
Americans how to put it on the screen in a new, "existential"
way'.

L'ADDITION
[THE PATSY]

1983. 87 mins
d. Denis Amar
sc. Amar, Jean-Pierre Bastide, Jean Curtelin
ph. Robert Fraisse
m. Jean-Claude Petit
p. Swanie/TF1/UGT-Top 1
with: Richard Berry, Richard Bohringer, Victoria Abril

A man (Berry) is imprisoned for a relatively minor offence and becomes the target of a sadistic guard (Bohringer) when wrongly accused of taking part in a breakout. A psychological thriller which lies somewhere between the fatalism of Marcel Carné and Jacques Prévert's pre-war 'poetic realist' films, and the paranoia of some recent American movies like Peter Yates's *An Innocent Man* (1989).

ALPHAVILLE

1965. bw. 98 mins.
d. Jean-Luc Godard
sc. Godard
ph. Raoul Coutard
m. Paul Misraki
p. Chaumiane/Filmstudio
with: Eddie Constantine, Anna Karina, Howard Vernon, Akim Tamiroff

Constantine returns in his 1950s rôle as the Peter Cheyney private eye, Lemmy Caution, sent on an inter-galactic mission to a city from which love and individuality have been banned by the dictator-scientist Von Braun (Vernon). Godard's film is about alienation, of course, and old B-movies; but also about modern Paris, which Coutard's camera superbly reinterprets as a threatening future world of glass and neon. Not a genre movie, but a film about genre movies.

L'AMOUR VIOLÉ
[RAPE OF LOVE]

1977. 110 mins.
d. Yannick Bellon
sc. Bellon
ph. Georges Barsky, Pierre William Glenn
m. Aram Sedefian
p. Equinoxe/Dragon/MK2
with: Nathalie Nell, Alain Fourès, Daniel Auteuil

A nurse (Nell) is the victim of a gang rape and starts to investigate the reasons behind it. She uncovers a recurrent theme in post-war thrillers: the banality of evil.

LES ANGES DU PÉCHÉ
[ANGELS OF THE STREETS]

1943. bw. 73 mins.
d. Robert Bresson
sc. Bresson, Jean Giraudoux, Père R. Bruckberger
ph. Philippe Agostini
m. Jean-Jacques Grünewald
ad. René Renoux
p. Synops/Roland Tual
with: Renée Faure, Jany Holt, Sylvie.

A nun (Faure) tries to rehabilitate a woman (Holt) who has been imprisoned to defend her lover. Based on the work of the convent of the Sisters of Béthany, the film is a remarkable first picture, introducing many of the themes that Bresson was to explore later in his career, notably in his questioning of conventional morality: the nun is a bourgeoise whose apparent humility and devotion are the outward signs of her inner pride and authoritarianism. Georges Sadoul (*Le Cinéma français*, Flammarion, Paris, 1962) called it 'a perfect stylistic exercise'.

L'ARGENT

1983. 84 mins.
d. Robert Bresson
sc. Bresson, from a story by Tolstoy
ph. Emmanuel Machuel, Pasqualino De Santis
m. J. S. Bach
p. Eos/Marion/FR3
with: Christian Patey, Sylvie van den Elsen, Michel Briguet.

Two schoolboys pass a forged note and the film follows the consequences of this act from mischief to murder. As in Bresson's earlier work, crime acts as the agent for spiritual redemption; and, though he criticizes the effects of money on social relations, he does not try to provide a sociological explanation for the actions of the characters: this is an austere universe, in which evil and original sin are present everywhere. The film won the award for Best Director at Cannes.

L'ARMÉE DES OMBRES
[THE ARMY IN THE SHADOWS]

1969. 140 mins.
d. Jean-Pierre Melville
sc. Melville
ph. Pierre Lhomme
m. Eric de Marsan
p. Corona/Fono Roma
with: Lino Ventura, Simone Signoret. Jean-Pierre Cassel, Paul Meurisse, Serge Reggiani

A resistance leader (Ventura) determines to discover who has betrayed him to the Gestapo. An account of the Lyon resistance which most critics identified (sometimes with disapproval) as essentially a gangster film: given Melville's status as a director in that genre, and the extent to which he drew on his wartime experiences for it, this has to be the prime example of the link between the two themes in post-war French cinema.

ASCENSEUR POUR L'ÉCHAFAUD
[LIFT TO THE SCAFFOLD]

1957. bw. 89 mins.
d. Louis Malle
sc. Malle, Roger Nimier from the novel by Noel Calef
ph. Henri Deca
m. Miles Davis
p. Nouvelles Editions de Films
with: Maurice Ronet, Jeanne Moreau, Georges Poujouly, Lino Ventura

An ex-paratrooper (Ronet) devises an ingenious plot to murder his boss with the help of the victim's wife (Moreau), but the plan goes awry when he gets stuck in the lift and his car is stolen; the wife wanders the streets waiting for him to telephone, while the young car thief kills a German tourist with Ronet's gun. Behind the implausible narrative, some critics detected references to contemporary events: 'the characters belong precisely to our time,' according to Armand Monjo (*L'Humanité*, Feb. 1, 1958). Malle's first film marked an important stage in the career of Jeanne Moreau, giving her her best acting role up to that time.

L'ASSASSIN HABITE AU 21

1942. bw. 90 mins
d. Henri-Georges Clouzot
sc. Clouzot, S. A. Steeman from Steeman's novel
ph. Armand Thirard
m. Maurice Yvain
ad. André Andreyev
p. Continental
with: Pierre Fresnay, Suzy Delair, Jean Tissier

A detective (Fresnay) and his assistant (Delair) investigate a murder in a boarding-house. Clouzot's first feature is a fairly routine comedy-thriller from a novel originally set in London (this explains some of the eccentricities of the characters). A good example of the traditional, 'least likely suspect' thriller, the subversive potential of which Clouzot was to develop in *Le Corbeau*.

L'ATTENTAT
[PLOT]

1972. 124 mins
d. Yves Boisset
sc. Jorge Semprun
ph. Ricardo Aronovich
m. Ennio Morricone
p. Transinter/Terza/Corona
with: Gian Maria Volonté, Jean-Louis Trintignant, Michel Piccoli, Jean Seberg, François Périer, Philippe Noiret

The CIA and the French secret service plot to dispose of a North African political exile (Volonté), with the unwitting help of a journalist (Trintignant). A conspiracy movie, based on the Ben Barka affair, which makes an effective thriller.

AU-DELÀ DES GRILLES
[THE WALLS OF MALAPAGA]

1949. bw. 91 mins.
d. René Clément
sc. Cesare Zavattini, Suso Cecchi D'Amico, Jean Aurenche, Pierre Bost
ph. Louis Page
m. Roman Vlad
ad. Piero Filippone
p. Guarini/Francinex
with: Jean Gabin, Isa Miranda, Vera Talchi

Pierre (Gabin), on the run after killing his mistress, escapes to Italy and meets a waitress (Miranda), with whom he falls in love: the film is basically a fatalistic love story, remarkable chiefly for the location work. Two of the leading scriptwriters of Italian Neo-Realism (Zavattini and Cecchi D'Amico) collaborated on the script with the two masters of the French well-made film (Aurenche and Bost) to give Gabin a final opportunity to play the character of the doomed criminal/hero which he had created in his great pre-war films. Clément won the award for Best Director at Cannes and Miranda that for Best Actress.

AUX YEUX DU MONDE
[AUTOBUS]

1991. 95 mins.
d. Eric Rochant
sc. Rochant
ph. Pierre Novion
m. Gérard Torikian
ad. Pascale Fenouillet
p. Alain Rocca/Les Prod. Lazennec/FR3/SGGC/La Générale d'Images
with: Yvan Attal, Kristin Scott-Thomas, Marc Berman, Charlotte Gainsbourg

To prove himself to his girlfriend (Gainsbourg), a young man (Attal) hi-jacks a school bus and, as he forces them to drive through the countryside, wins the sympathy of the schoolteacher (Scott-Thomas) and driver (Berman). After his feature debut with *Un monde sans pitié* (1989), Rochant made an equally simple and touching story in which the threatening criminal is gradually perceived by his victims as just a confused and lonely young man.

L'AVEU
[THE CONFESSION]

1970. 160 mins.
d. Costa-Gavras
sc. Jorge Semprun from the book by Artur London
ph. Raoul Coutard
ad. Bernard Evein
p. Robert Dorfmann, Bertrand Javal/Corona/Pomereus/Serena
with: Yves Montand, Simone Signoret, Michel Vitold

The arrest and torture of the Czech foreign minister, London (Montand) in 1951. Costa-Gavras' attack on the Kafkaesque horrors of the Stalinist show trials was bound to arouse controversy in the wake of the 'Prague Spring' and the Russian invasion of 1968. It came under attack from some left-wingers, particularly in the communist press (François Maurin, *L'Humanité*, April 29, 1970) for its political tendencies and simplifications, though *Les Lettres françaises* (Marc Capdenac, May 13, 1970) was favourable. Most critics praised Montand's acting, though some (especially in America) found the politics confused. The genre elements (even of a 'political thriller', like *Z*) are almost entirely absent: a 'political prison movie', perhaps.

LA BALANCE

1981. 102 mins.
d. Bob Swaim
sc. Swaim, M. Fabiani
ph. Bernard Zitzermann
m. Roland Bocquet
p. Ariane/A2
with: Nathalie Baye, Philippe Léotard, Richard Berry, Maurice Ronet

After an informer is murdered in the street, a member of the Brigades Territoriales (Berry) plans to get the evidence he needs to nail a drug baron (Ronet) by exploiting the love affair between a petty criminal (Léotard) and a prostitute (Baye). One of the best thrillers of its period, making good use of locations in Belleville and convincingly developing a love relationship which seems likely to be as doomed as those in the pre-war 'poetic realist' movies.

BANDE À PART
[BAND OF OUTSIDERS]

1964. bw. 95 mins.
d. Jean-Luc Godard
sc. Godard, from the novel *Fool's Gold* by Dolores Hitchens
ph. Raoul Coutard
m. Michel Legrand
p. Anouchka/Orsay
with: Anna Karina, Sami Frey, Claude Brasseur

A girl (Karina) joins up with two toughs (Frey, Brasseur) and they plan a robbery. Play-acting the gangster spills over into reality: 'like a reverie of a gangster movie . . . ,' according to Pauline Kael, ' — a mixture of the gangster film virtues (loyalty, daring) with innocence, amorality, lack of equilibrium.' Godard described the two men as 'suburban cousins of Belmondo in *A bout de souffle*'; and the film has the same New Wave verve combined with a refusal to take anything serious seriously.

BOB LE FLAMBEUR
[BOB THE GAMBLER]

1955. bw. 100 mins.
d. Jean-Pierre Melville
sc. Melville, Auguste Le Breton
ph. Henri Decaë
m. Eddie Barclay, Jean Boyer
p. Jenner/Cyme/Play Art/OGC

with: Roger Duchesne, Isabelle Corey, Daniel Cauchy, Howard Vernon

A gambler and crook (Duchesne) plans a robbery on a casino. The action of the film takes place between nightfall and daybreak in Montmartre, while the music and camera style foreshadow the New Wave; but this is also a documentary-style American *film noir* relocated to France.

BORSALINO

1970. 128 mins.
d. Jacques Deray
sc. Deray, Jean-Claude Carrière, Claude Sautet, Jean Cau
ph. Jean-Jacques Tarbes
m. Claude Bolling
p. Delon/Adel/Marianne/Mars
with: Jean-Paul Belmondo, Alain Delon, Michel Bouquet, Catherine Rouvel

Two small-time crooks (Belmondo, Delon) rise in the Marseille underworld during the 1930s by controlling meat supplies. A jolly gangster-plus-buddy movie, with an attractive score and two stars who brought memories of earlier roles and seem to be enjoying these, too. A period setting made it easier to sympathize with their activities: safely in the past, they could not be construed as a threat. The inevitable sequel, *Borsalino & Co* (1974) was less successful.

LE BOUCHER
[THE BUTCHER]

1969. 94 mins.
d. Claude Chabrol
sc. Chabrol
ph. Jean Rabier
m. Pierre Jansen
ad. Guy Littaye

p. André Génovès/Films de la Boétie/Euro International
with: Jean Yanne, Stéphane Audran

The schoolmistress (Audran) in a small town in Périgord is shyly courted by the local butcher (Yanne) and the pair are drawn together by loneliness. But the little community is being terrorized by a sadistic killer. Clearly influenced by Hitchcock (notably *Shadow of a Doubt*), this is a study in sexual repression and a reflection on civilization and savagery, the elegant architecture of the setting (in reality the village of Trémolat) being only a step from the woods and prehistoric caves just beyond its borders. *Le Figaro* called this the best French film since the Liberation, and it was generally praised as Chabrol's masterpiece. Its great virtues are the simplicity and resonance of the narrative, and Chabrol's ultimate refusal to 'explain' the mystery of the central character.

BUFFET FROID
[COLD CUTS]

1979. 95 mins.
d. Bertrand Blier
sc. Blier
ph. Jean Penzer
m. Brahms
p. Sara/A2
with: Bernard Blier, Gérard Depardieu, Jean Carmet

A penknife belonging to a young man (Depardieu) is used as a murder weapon and the police inspector (Blier) on the case is naturally suspicious. More murders follow. A typically picaresque work by its director, developing the relationship between the two men to uncover the hypocrisies of bourgeois society, with a good dose of tasteless black comedy.

CASQUE D'OR
[GOLDEN MARIE]

1952. bw. 96 mins.
d. Jacques Becker
sc. Becker, Jacques Companeez
ph. Robert Le Febvre
m. Georges van Parys
ad. Jean d'Eaubonne
p. Speva/Paris
with: Simone Signoret, Serge Reggiani, Claude Dauphin, Raymond Bussières, Gaston Modot

In Belleville, in 1904, a workman, Manda (Reggiani), falls for the girlfriend (Signoret) of an 'apache', whom he accidentally kills in a fight. The gang leader (Dauphin) denounces an innocent man (Bussières) and Manda hands himself over to the police. Becker said: 'I don't like wrongdoers; a "perfect crime" is a matter for psychiatrists . . . I'm interested in human beings.' Perhaps Signoret's finest role, in a brilliantly constructed story making excellent use of the contrast between the dangers of the city and the idyllic countryside to which the two lovers escape for a brief moment of happiness. The Belleville setting at the turn of the century can be compared with the use of the same district in films like *La Balance*, which also explores its seedy atmosphere as now a mainly immigrant quarter. The film was not as successful in France as in Britain, where Signoret won the British Film Academy Award: Dilys Powell called it 'one of the best films I have seen in ten years', speaking of 'brutality and coarseness irradiated by tenderness' and 'the qualities which make a classic' (September 1952). The simple narrative, beautifully edited and acted, makes it a masterpiece.

LE CAVE SE REBIFFE
[THE COUNTERFEITERS]

1961. bw. 98 mins.
d. Gilles Grangier
sc. Grangier, Albert Simonin, Michel Audiard
ph. Louis Page
m. Francis Lemarque, Michel Legrand
p. Cité/Compagnia Cinematografica Mondiale
with: Jean Gabin, Martine Carol, Maurice Biraud, Bernard Blier

A retired criminal (Gabin) is persuaded to mastermind a scam, but plans to doublecross his associates with the help of the forger (Biraud). A minor comedy-thriller, with Gabin in one of his typical later roles.

LE CERCLE ROUGE

1970. 150 mins.
d. Jean-Pierre Melville
sc. Melville
ph. Henri Decaë
m. Eric de Marsan
p. Corona/Selenia
with: Alain Delon, Yves Montand, François Périer, André Bourvil, Gian Maria Volonté

Bourvil, in his last film, plays a police inspector, with Delon and Montand as the two gangsters. Melville explores the old theme of the relationship between criminals and police. but the outcome was a failure in Britain and America because of the incompetence of the English-language version.

LE CHAT ET LA SOURIS
[CAT AND MOUSE]

1975. 108 mins.
d. Claude Lelouch
sc. Lelouch
ph. Jean Collomb
m. Francis Lai
p. Les Films 13
with: Michèle Morgan, Serge Reggiani, Jean-Pierre Aumont

An industrialist (Aumont) is murdered and the police inspector (Reggiani) suspects his widow (Morgan). As one would expect from Lelouch, a glossy commercial thriller.

LE CLAN DES SICILIENS
[THE SICILIAN CLAN]

1968. 120 mins.
d. Henri Verneuil
sc. Verneuil, José Giovanni, Pierre Pelégri
ph. Henri Decaë
m. Ennio Morricone
p. Fox-Europa/Films du Siècle
with: Jean Gabin, Alain Delon, Lino Ventura

A criminal (Delon) escapes from jail and teams up for a robbery with an aging Mafia boss (Gabin); but they fall out over the younger man's affair with the godfather's daughter-in-law. Three heavies (Gabin, Delon and Ventura) meet, but the film remains a fairly lightweight example of the Mafia genre.

COMPARTIMENT TUEURS
[THE SLEEPING CAR MURDERS]

1965. bw. 95 mins.
d. Costa-Gavras
sc. Costa-Gavras, Sébastien Japrisot from Japrisot's novel
ph. Jean Tournier
m. Michel Magne
p. Julien Derode/PECF
with: Yves Montand, Simone Signoret, Pierre Mondy, Catherine Allégret, Michel Piccoli, Claude Mann

A woman is murdered on the Marseille-Paris express and Inspector Gazzi (Montand) investigates with the help of his assistant (Mann); then the witnesses start to die. Costa-Gavras' first film was a success, though more abroad than in France. Richard Davis (*Films and Filming*, Dec. 1966) called it cool, efficient and heartless — 'a direct harking back to the vintage years of the French whodunnit'.

LE CORBEAU
[THE RAVEN]

1943. bw. 92 mins.
d. Henri-Georges Clouzot
sc. Louis Chavance
ph. Nicholas Hayer
m. Tony Aubain
p. Continental
with: Pierre Fresnay, Ginette Leclerc, Pierre Larquey, Hélène Manson, Micheline Francey

When a small town is plagued by poison-pen letters, a doctor (Fresnay) and two women (Leclerc, Manson) fall successively under suspicion. A classic of the 'least-likely suspect' movie, remade by Otto Preminger as *The Thirteenth Letter* (1951), and inspired by a real case in Tulle. It achieved the distinction of coming under vicious attack from all quarters. The Catholic Church hated it and its cinema watchdogs warned audiences to avoid the film at all costs. The Right hated it, *L'Action française* (Oct. 3, 1943) saying that it infringed the principles of the most elementary morality. The Resistance called it pro-German propaganda and banned it for two years after the Liberation. If nothing else, it hit a nerve. Dilys Powell (Feb. 1954) found Clouzot's view of human nature 'savagely pessimistic'.

COUP DE TORCHON
[CLEAN SLATE]

1981. 128 mins.
d. Bertrand Tavernier
sc. Tavernier, Jean Aurenche from the novel *Pop 1280* by Jim Thompson
ph. Pierre-William Glenn
m. Philippe Sarde
p. Les Films de la Tour/A2/Little Bear
with: Philippe Noiret, Isabelle Huppert, Jean-Pierre Marielle, Stéphane Audran

After 'legitimately' killing two pimps, a colonial law officer (Noiret) in pre-war West Africa starts to eliminate racist Europeans — and anyone else he dislikes, including his wife (Audran) and mistress (Huppert). Tavernier relocates Jim Thompson's thriller (which Alain Corneau had considered filming) from the American Deep South to the French colonies, to make the story a figure for the lawlessness and insanity of the colonial situation.

DÉDÉE D'ANVERS
[WOMAN OF ANTWERP]

1948. bw. 95 mins
d. Yves Allégret
sc. Allégret, Jacques Sigurd
ph. Jean Bourgoin

m. Jacques Besse
p. Sacha Gordine/André Paulvé
with: Simone Signoret, Marcel Pagliero, Bernard Blier, Marcel
Dalio

A prostitute (Signoret) falls in love with a sailor (Pagliero),
arousing the anger of her pimp (Blier). A post-war melodrama which attempts to recreate the doom-laden atmosphere of the Carné-Prévert films, it marked the high point of
Signoret's collaboration with her then husband, Allégret.

DÉTECTIVE

1985. 95 mins.
d. Jean-Luc Godard
sc. Godard, Anne-Marie Miéville, Alain Sarde, Philippe Setbon
ph. Bruno Nuytten
m. Wagner, Chopin, Honegger, Chabrier, Ornette Coleman,
Jean Schwarz
p. Alain Sarde/Sara/JLG Films
with: Nathalie Baye, Claude Brasseur, Johnny Hallyday, Laurent Terzieff, Jean-Pierre Léaud, Alain Cuny

Different groups of people (Mafia, boxers, detectives) gather
in a hotel where a murder was committed two years earlier.
Asked why she agreed to make the film, Baye said that
Godard told her the story. 'Fantastic. Three weeks later he
told me another completely different story — just as fantastic.' Typical late Godard, with an incomprehensible plot,
and the usual omelette of references to B-movies, literature
and so on — brilliant or pointless, according to taste. A film
about the limitations of post-modernist self-awareness, perhaps.

DEUX HOMMES DANS MANHATTAN
[TWO MEN IN MANHATTAN]

1959. bw. 84 mins.
d. Jean-Pierre Melville
sc. Melville
ph. Melville, Nicolas Hayer
m. Christian Chevalier, Martial Solal
p. Belfort/Alter
with: Melville, Pierre Grasset, Christiane Eudes, Monique Hennessy

Two French journalists (Melville, Grasset) investigate the mysterious disappearance of a diplomat by interviewing the women in his life. Exteriors shot with a hand-held camera in New York and the whole a tribute to the city and to American movies. As *noir* as you can get, in one sense, because all the action takes place at night, except for the finale as day breaks.

LE DEUXIÈME SOUFFLE
[SECOND BREATH]

1966. bw. 150 mins.
d. Jean-Pierre Melville
sc. Melville
ph. Marcel Combes
m. Bernard Gérard
p. Montaigne
with: Lino Ventura, Paul Meurisse, Raymond Pellegrin, Christine Fabrega

After his escape from jail, a gangster (Ventura) takes part in a highway robbery, but is then tricked by a police inspector (Meurisse) into betraying the other members of the gang. Melville explores two fundamental themes: the mutually dependent relationship between policeman and criminal, and the criminal's code of honour (compare, for example, Bob Swaim's *La Balance*). Of the character played by Ventura, he said: 'though he is a menace to society, he has preserved a kind of purity.'

LES DIABOLIQUES
[THE FIENDS]

1954. bw. 114 mins.
d. Henri-Georges Clouzot
sc. Clouzot, Jérôme Géronimi, Frédéric Grendel, René Masson from the novel by Boileau-Narcejac
ph. Armand Thirard
m. Georges van Parys
p. Filmsonor/Vera
with: Simone Signoret, Vera Clouzot, Paul Meurisse, Charles Vanel

The wife (Vera Clouzot) and mistress (Signoret) of a schoolteacher (Meurisse) plot to kill him, but the body disappears. Or does it? A notorious thriller, the ending of which is one shock after another — each more improbable than the last. Pauline Kael found 'overtones and undertones of strange, tainted pleasures and punishments . . . Preposterously sensational as all this is, there is no doubt that thinking about it makes one feel queasy and sordid and scared.' British critics reacted strongly to it when it was first released (after a good deal of publicity urging audiences not to give away the ending); but Jacques Rivette found Clouzot and his contemporaries 'sickening' for other reasons: 'they are corrupted, corrupted by money . . . What is most lacking in French cinema is a spirit of poverty' (*Cahiers du cinéma*, round-table discussion, May 1957). Just the sort of commercial film, in other words, that French directors in the 1950s did well.

1981. 117 mins.
d. Jean-Jacques Beneix
sc. Beneix, Jean van Hamme
ph. Philippe Rousselot
m. Vladimir Cosma
p. Galaxie/Greenwich
with: Frédéric Andrei, Wilhelminia Wiggins Fernandez, Roland Bertin. Thuy An Luu

A messenger boy (Andrei) records an aria by an opera singer (Fernandez) and finds that his life is threatened by possession of the cassette which is confused with another that has been slipped into his bag. Glossily made, fast-moving thriller, with nowhere to go and nothing to do except quote extensively from earlier examples of the genre. 'Beneix may not be interested in what's underneath,' Pauline Kael, 'but he has a great feeling for surfaces . . . Every shot seems to have a shaft of wit.' Much admired on its release.

DOCTEUR PETIOT

1990. bw/col 102 mins.
d. Christian de Chalonge
sc. Chalonge, Dominique Garnier
ph. Patrick Blossier
m. Michel Portal
ad. Yves Brover
p. MS/Sara
with: Michel Serrault, Berangère Bonvoisin, Pierre Romans, Zbigniew Horoks

During the German Occupation, Dr. Petiot (Serrault) lures Jewish victims of Nazi persecution to his apartment in Paris, with the promise that he can help them escape to Argentina. There he tells them that they must be vaccinated and applies a fatal injection, watching them as they die, then stealing their belongings. Based on the real case of a man guillotined in 1946, this is not a conventional biography, but a disturb-ing study of a psychopath who is capable of devotion to saving lives as well as taking them, and suffers from an apparent ability to play any part except himself. The director and designer make effective use of the visual lan-guage of German Expressionism to evoke the atmosphere of the Occupation and the insanities of the time.

LE DOULOS
[THE FINGER MAN]

1962. bw. 108 mins.
d. Jean-Pierre Melville
sc. Melville
ph. Nicolas Hayer
m. Paul Misraki
p. Rome-Paris Films/CCC
with: Jean-Paul Belmondo, Serge Reggiani, Monique Hennessy, Michel Piccoli, Jean Desailly

A man just released from prison (Reggiani) and living with his girlfriend (Hennessy) organizes a robbery with Silien (Belmondo), but everything goes wrong. Melville's film deals with his favourite themes of 'honour among thieves', love and betrayal. The French critics were divided about this enigmatic piece, with its inconclusive ending.

DU RIFIFI CHEZ LES HOMMES
[RIFIFI]

1955. bw. 116 mins.
d. Jules Dassin
sc. Dassin, René Wheeler, Auguste le Breton from Le Breton's novel
ph. Philippe Agostini
m. Georges Auric
p. Indus/Pathé/Prima

with: Jean Servais, Carl Mohner, Robert Manuel, Marie Sabouret, Magali Noël, Dassin

Four jewel thieves (Servais, Mohner, Manuel, Dassin) plan an ingenious robbery, then clash with another gang over the loot. Famous because of the suspenseful 22-minute sequence of the robbery, with no dialogue and only 'natural' sound effects which, as Sadoul points out, in his *Dictionnaire des films*, is made with an element of wry humour. The documentary realism and the moral (crime doesn't pay) guaranteed critical and public success. Dassin worked in France after being blacklisted in the United States.

L'ÉTOILE DU NORD
[THE NORTHERN STAR]

1982. 124 mins.
d. Pierre Granier-Deferre
sc. Granier-Deferre, Jean Aurenche, Michel Grisolia from Simenon's novel *Le Locataire*
ph. Pierre-William Glenn
m. Philippe Sarde
p. Sara/A2
with: Philippe Noiret, Simone Signoret

A man (Noiret) takes refuge in a Belgian boarding-house in the 1930s, and talks about his past life in Egypt, having apparently forgotten that he committed a murder on the express train from Paris. The second (and confused) re-make of this Simenon novel.

LES FANATIQUES
[THE FANATICS]

1957. bw. 92 mins.
d. Alex Joffé
sc. Joffé, Jean Levitte

ph. L. H. Burel
m. Paul Misraki
p. Cinégraph/CGC/Regent
with: Pierre Fresnay, Michel Auclair, Grégoire Aslan, Françoise Fabian

Two assassins (Fresnay, Auclair) agree to blow up a small plane carrying a South American dictator (Aslan), but face a crisis of conscience when he changes to a scheduled flight, involving other passengers. An early political thriller on a moral dilemma that was to become more topical over the next decade.

FANTÔMAS

1964. 105 mins.
d. André Hunebelle
sc. Jean Halain, Pierre Foucaud
ph. Marcel Grignon
m. Michel Magne
p. PAC/SNEG/PCM
with: Jean Marais, Louis de Funès, Mylène Demongeot, Marie-Hélène Arnaud

Not a remake, but a homage to Louis Feuillade's famous silent serial of 1913, which brings together the arch-criminal, the police inspector and the investigative journalist — three essential characters in the crime movie.

LES FANTÔMES DU CHAPELIER
[THE HATTER'S GHOSTS]

1982. 129 mins.
d. Claude Chabrol
sc. Chabrol from a novel by Simenon
ph. Jean Rabier
m. Matthieu Chabrol
p. Horizon/A2/SFPC

with: Michel Serrault, Charles Aznavour, Monique Chaumette

A provincial hatter (Serrault) maintains a façade of respectability while embarking on a career as a murderer. Nothing particularly original about the theme of this film, which is chiefly remarkable for Serrault's performance and the recreation of the small-town atmosphere.

LA FEMME INFIDÉLE
[THE UNFAITHFUL WIFE]

1968. 98 mins
d. Claude Chabrol
sc. Chabrol
ph. Jean Rabier
m. Pierre Jansen
ad. Guy Littaye
p. Les Films de la Boétie/Cinegai
with: Stéphane Audran, Michel Bouquet, Maurice Ronet

In a fit of rage, a husband (Bouquet) kills the lover (Ronet) of his wife (Audran). And, Chabrol suggests, saves his marriage. Accused of cynicism at the time when it was released, this is in fact an analysis of bourgeois relationships and an ironic reflexion on fidelity and infidelity.

GOUPI MAINS ROUGES
[IT HAPPENED AT THE INN]

1943. bw. 95 mins.
d. Jacques Becker
sc. Becker, Pierre Véry
ph. Pierre Montazel, Jean Bourgoin
m. Jean Alfaro
p. Minerva
with: Fernand Ledoux, Georges Rollin, Blanchette Brunoy, Robert Le Vigan

Four generations of the Goupi family live in the same village in the Charentais. When one of them is murdered, Goupi 'Mains Rouges' (Ledoux) goes after his killer (Le Vigan). A mixture of black comedy and precise — almost documentary — study of peasant life, which Sadoul likened to the films of Jean Renoir, though the more obvious comparison is with extraordinary documentary-drama *Farrebique* (1946). The interest in peasant subjects was encouraged during the Occupation, but did not get quite the treatment in either of these films that Pétainists would have welcomed, with their nostalgia for the honest virtues of rural life. Goupi was not released abroad until some time after the war, when Dilys Powell regretted that it had not had the success it deserved with British audiences.

L'HORLOGER DE SAINT-PAUL
[THE WATCHMAKER OF ST PAUL]

1973. 105 mins.
d. Bertrand Tavernier
sc. Tavernier, Jean Aurenche, Pierre Bost
ph. Pierre-William Glenn
m. Philippe Sarde
p. Lira
with: Philippe Noiret, Jean Rochefort, Sylvain Rougerie, Christine Pascal

A young man (Rougerie) and his girlfriend (Pascal) are hunted for the murder of an industrialist. When he is arrested, he refuses to see his father (Noiret), who turns to the police inspector (Rochefort) to help him understand the motives for the crime. In the aftermath of 1968, Tavernier's first film explores the generation gap against a finely-drawn picture of life in Lyon. Critics have pointed to his use of the scriptwriters Aurenche and Bost, whose names stand for the 1950s films hated by the New Wave. Jill Forbes sees the film as an argument for reconciliation, but is unconvinced by the elements of *film noir* in what she describes as an attempt 'to synthesize the French and American traditions of the 1950s'.

INSPECTEUR LAVARDIN

1986. 103 mins.
d. Claude Chabrol
sc. Chabrol, Dominique Roulet
ph. Jean Rabier
m. Matthieu Chabrol
p. MK2/A2/TV Suisse Romande
with: Jean Poiret, Jean-Claude Brialy, Bernadette Lafont

The inspector (Poiret) from *Poulet au vinaigre* is sent to investigate the murder of a personality involved in banning a play for blasphemy, only to find that the widow (Lafont) is an old flame and the household a bizarre collection of eccentrics. Highly entertaining comedy-thriller about the policeman as God.

JEU DE MASSACRE
[COMIC STRIP HERO/THE KILLING GAME]

1967. 95 mins.
d. Alain Jessua
sc. Jessua
ph. Jacques Robin
m. Jacques Loussier
p. Francinor/Coficitel/AJ/Films Modernes
with: Jean-Pierre Cassel, Claudine Auger, Michel Duchaussoy

A writer of comic strips (Cassel) and his wife (Auger), who illustrates them, are disturbed by the arrival of a stranger (Duchaussoy) claiming to be one of his heroes. Reality and fantasy combine in an exploration of a genre (*illustrés*, drawn for the film by Guy Pellaert) that was becoming increasingly varied and respectable in France at the time.

1963. bw. 95 mins.
d. Georges Franju
sc. Jacques Champreux, Francis Lacassin
ph. Marcel Fradetal
m. Maurice Jarre
ad. Gilbert Natot
p. Comptoir Français du Film/Filmes
with: Channing Pollock, Francine Bergé, Edith Scob, Michel Vitold

A dishonest banker (Vitold) is kidnapped by Judex (Pollock) who wants revenge for his mother, whom the man has driven to suicide. A revival of Feuillade's serial of 1916 and far more successful than Hunebelle's *Fantômas*. Franju draws on the tradition of surrealism, dada and expressionism for what Sadoul called 'an outstanding success, a tribute that is both respectful and full of humour'. British audiences were bemused by it when it was first given a limited release in London.

LE JUGE ET L'ASSASSIN
[THE JUDGE AND THE ASSASSIN]

1976. 110 mins.
d. Bertrand Tavernier
sc. Tavernier, Jean Aurenche, Pierre Bost
ph. Pierre-William Glenn
m. Philippe Sarde
p. Raymond Davos/Lira
with: Philippe Noiret, Michel Galabru, Isabelle Huppert, Jean Claude Brialy, Yves Robert

In the Ardèche, in the late nineteenth century, a man (Galabru) is arrested for a series of sex murders and the judge (Noiret) has to rule on his sanity. The theme of the relationship between criminal and representative of the law is given a new dimension. The relativity (social and historical) of definitions of madness was a question that interested historians, in particular Michel Foucault, and Tavernier reflects this concern: society's need for absolutes, and the impossibility of establishing them.

JUSTE AVANT LA NUIT
[JUST BEFORE NIGHTFALL]

1971. 107 mins.
d. Claude Chabrol
sc. Chabrol
ph. Jean Rabier
m. Pierre Jansen
p. Films de la Boétie/Columbia
with: Michel Bouquet, Stéphane Audran, François Périer

A small-town bourgeois (Bouquet) murders his mistress, the wife of his best friend (Périer), then confesses; but no one is prepared to judge him. A sort of reversal of *La Femme infidèle*, picking up a similar theme about the middle classes, guilt and the need to keep up appearances; with a sub-plot about a robbery.

JUSTICE EST FAITE
[JUSTICE IS DONE/LET JUSTICE BE DONE]

1950. bw. 105 mins.
d. André Cayatte
sc. Cayatte, Charles Spaak
ph. Jean Bourgoin
m. Raymond Legrand
p. Silver Films
with: Claude Nollier, Michel Auclair, Valentine Tessier

Else (Nollier) goes on trial for euthanasia, and the film looks both at the court proceedings and at the personal lives of the jury members. This bitingly satirical analysis of the legal system is the best work by Cayatte, who specialized in social problem dramas: both he and Spaak had trained as lawyers and set out to show justice as purely a lottery. It won awards for Best Film at Venice and Berlin.

L. 627

1992. 145 mins.
d. Bertrand Tavernier
sc. Tavernier, Michel Alexandre
ph. Alain Choquart
m. Philippe Sarde
ad. Guy-Claude François
p. Little Bear/Les Films Alain Sarde
with: Didier Bezace, Charlotte Kady, Philippe Torreton, Nils Tavernier

Transferred from the Seventh Division for insubordination, 'Lulu' Marguet (Bezace) finds himself in the drugs squad, where life is a mixture of stake-outs, chases, arrests and paperwork. Tavernier describes the policeman's lot, centered on a sympathetic figure who is dedicated to ridding society of the evil of drugs. The language and settings are convincing, but the film did not please the police authorities (see Tavernier's diary of the year 1992 in *Projections 2*, published by Faber).

LANDRU
[BLUEBEARD]

1962. 115 mins.
d. Claude Chabrol
sc. Chabrol, Françoise Sagan
ph. Jean Rabier
m. Pierre Jansen
ad. Jacques Saulnier
p. CC Champion/Rome-Paris Films
with: Charles Denner, Michèle Morgan, Danielle Darrieux, Hildegard Knef

Based on the true story of a murderer, also dramatized by Chaplin in *Monsieur Verdoux* (1947): Landru (Denner) charms his female victims, then kills them for their money. The film was not a box office success and critics found the central performance too loaded with caricature. Robin Wood describes Landru as a central figure in the Chabrol universe and writes: 'the action presents Landru . . . in a whole series of roles: paterfamilias, sexual pervert, devoted and apparently normal lover. The pervert doesn't cancel out the normal man, or vice versa. . . He goes to the guillotine assured of his own essential innocence, the secret of his identity intact.' Compare *Docteur Petiot* and the fictional character of Popaul in Chabrol's *Le Boucher*.

LA LUNE DANS LE CANIVEAU
[THE MOON IN THE GUTTER]

1983. 130 mins.
d. Jean-Jacques Beineix
sc. Beineix from a novel by David Goodis
ph. Philippe Rousselot
m. Gabriel Yared
p. Gaumont/TF1/SFPC/Opera Film Produzione
with: Gérard Depardieu, Nastassja Kinski, Vittorio Mezzogiorno, Victoria Abril

A working man (Depardieu) hunts the man who drove his sister to suicide and becomes involved with a rich girl (Kinski), suspecting her brother (Mezzogiorno) of responsibility. Arty, hated by the critics and by Depardieu, who called it 'a thriller preoccupied with its own navel'.

MAIGRET TEND UN PIÈGE
[MAIGRET SETS A TRAP]

1957. bw. 120 mins.
d. Jean Delannoy
sc. Michel Audiard from the novel by Simenon
ph. Louis Page
m. Paul Misraki
p. Intermondial/J.-P. Guibert/Jolly
with: Jean Gabin, Annie Girardot, Jean Desailly

Women are being murdered and Maigret sets out to capture the killer. A great success in France, chiefly because of Gabin, as Dilys Powell pointed out (Aug. 1959), using the film's London release as an excuse to analyze the appeal of its star: 'Time may slacken the face and torso, but the audience still agonizes with Maigret as he is balked; still longs to tweak his sleeve and point to a clue; and still thinks Madame Maigret a pretty lucky woman.' Otherwise, the film was merely enjoyable and efficient.

LA MARIÉE ÉTAIT EN NOIR
[THE BRIDE WORE BLACK]

1967. 107 mins.
d. François Truffaut
sc. Truffaut, Jean-Louis Richard from the novel by William Irish
ph. Raoul Coutard
m. Bernard Herrmann
ad. Pierre Guffroy
p. Les Films du Carrosse/Artistes Associés/Dino De Laurentis
with: Jeanne Moreau, Claude Rich, Jean-Claude Brialy, Michel Bouquet

The widow (Moreau) of a man shot on his wedding day progressively eliminates his killers. An obvious tribute to Hitchcock, the film offers us a disturbing central character, while at the same time making us accomplices in the heroine's crimes.

MASQUES

1987. 100 mins.
d. Claude Chabrol
sc. Chabrol, Odile Barski
ph. Jean Rabier
m. Matthieu Chabrol
p. MK2/A2
with: Philippe Noiret, Robin Renucci, Bernadette Lafont, Anne Brochet

A writer (Renucci) arrives in a country house to interview a TV personality (Noiret) whose sister has disappeared, and finds that everyone in the family is living a double life. Chabrol on his favourite ground: the nastiness behind the bourgeois façade — but even he is showing some signs of tiring.

MAUVAIS SANG
[THE NIGHT IS YOUNG]

1986. 119 mins.
d. Léos Carax
sc. Carax
ph. Jean-Yves Escoffier
m. Prokofiev, Britten, Aznavour
p. Les Films Plainchant/Soprofilms/FR3
with: Denis Lavant, Juliette Binoche, Michel Piccoli

A small-time thief and con artist (Lavant) becomes involved in a plot to steal a drug which is the only remedy against a virus that kills those who pretend to be in love. An obvious metaphor for AIDS, this is an undeniably stylish sci-fi thriller, with some enchanting colour photography and a general air of youthful enthusiasm, but a plot so complex,

and so obliquely told, that it leaves the impression of having
no content at all.

MAX ET LES FERAILLEURS
[MAX]

1971. 110 mins.
d. Claude Sautet
sc. Sautet, Claude Néron from Néron's novel
ph. René Mathelin
m. Philippe Sarde
p. Lira/Sonocam
with: Michel Piccoli, Romy Schneider, Bernard Fresson, François Périer, George Wilson

A police inspector (Piccoli) sets out on a private scheme to
bring criminals to justice, but falls in love with the mistress
(Schneider) of a thief. A competently made film on an
unusual theme, notable chiefly for its exploration of the
characters.

LA MÔME VERT-DE-GRIS
[POISON IVY]

1952. bw.
d. Bernard Borderie
sc. Jacques Vilfrid from the novels by Peter Cheyney
with: Eddie Constantine, Dominique Wilms

The first in a successful, self-consciously Anglo-Saxon
B-movie series intended mainly for the home market. The
character of Lemmy Caution (Constantine) reappeared in
Cet homme est dangereux (1953, Jean Sacha), *Les Femmes s'en
balancent* (1954, Borderie), *Ca va barder* (1954, John Berry), *Je
suis un sentimental* (1955, Berry) and others, surviving into the
1960s in *Lemmy pour les dames* (1961, Borderie). Like James
Bond, he rapidly became a parody of himself and the genre;

but the public didn't mind. One of the few that reached foreign screens was *Ca va barder* (roughly, 'There's trouble brewing'), which was released in the United States as *There Goes Barder*.

MONSIEUR HIRE

1989. 80 mins.
d. Patrice Leconte
sc. Leconte, Patrick Dewolf from the novel *Les Fiancailles de M. Hire* by Simenon
ph. Denis Lenoir
m. Michael Nyman
ad/ Ivan Maussion
p. Philippe Carcassonne/René Cleitman
with: Michel Blanc, Sandrine Bonnaire, Luc Thuillier, André Wilms

After a young girl is murdered, suspicion falls on Hire (Blanc), a lonely tailor who spends his time spying on the girl (Bonnaire) in the apartment across the courtyard as she undresses or makes love with her boyfriend (Thuillier). Then she notices him and comes over to confront him. Beautifully shot — the scenes of Hire watching at his window seem to be visually dictated by the rhythms of Nyman's music — and superbly acted, this is a story of *amour fou*, a reflexion on the voyeuristic rôle of the audience and an exploration of stereotypes of innocence and guilt. Simenon's novel had previously been adapted by Julien Duvivier as *Panique* (1946; q.v.). Leconte described Simenon as 'a false friend' for a film-maker, because his books are full of what appear to be 'visual' images, and said that he had set out to avoid any clear indication of period or location. A highly engaging and subtly disturbing film.

NIKITA

1990. 117 mins.
d. Luc Besson
sc. Besson
ph. Thierry Arbogast
m. Eric Serra
ad. Dan Weil
p. Films du Loup/Gaumont/Cecchi Gora/Tiger
with: Anne Parillaud, Jean-Hugues Anglade, Tchéky Karyo, Jeanne Moreau

A violent criminal (Parillaud) is captured after a robbery, sentenced to life imprisonment for murder, declared dead and recruited as an assassin by the secret service. The movie demands a great deal of Anne Parillaud in the part of an uncontrollable psychopath driven by a primitive hatred of society, who is capable of being tamed by her boss (Karyo) and of showing tenderness to her lover (Anglade). Geoff Andrews, writing in the *Time Out Film Guide*, observed 'there is for once an emotional undertow to Besson's visual pyrotechnics'; and the film's designer violence was certainly successful with its audience. On the surface, it has everything: action, sex, studiously beautiful colour photography, a dynamic and intriguing heroine . . . The trouble is, it's all on the surface.

NOUS SOMMES TOUS DES ASSASSINS
[WE ARE ALL MURDERERS]

1952. bw. 95 mins.
d. André Cayatte
sc. Cayatte, Charles Spaak
ph. Jean Bourgoin
m. Raymond Legrand
p. UGC
with: Mouloudji, Raymond Pellegrin, Antoine Balpêtre, Paul Frankeur

A former *résistant* (Mouloudji) is condemned to death for killing a policeman. A worthy and effective plea against the death penalty, resting its case on the agony of the man's last days and the obscenity of the ritual leading up to the guillotine. It won a special jury prize at Cannes in 1952 and, like Lelouch's *La Vie, l'amour, la mort* (1969), helped to open up a debate on the issue. The death penalty was not finally abolished in France until the 1980s.

ON NE MEURT QUE DEUX FOIS
[HE DIED WITH HIS EYES OPEN]

1985. 106 mins.
d. Jacques Deray
sc. Deray, Michel Audiard from the novel by Robin Cook
ph. Jean Penzer
m. Claude Bolling
p. Swaine/TF1
with: Michel Serrault, Charlotte Rampling, Elisabeth Depardieu

An inspector (Serrault), investigating the mysterious death of a pianist, becomes obsessed with the victim's mistress (Rampling), doubting her confession to the murder. Despite a lot of mystification in the plot, a conventional thriller, differing from many earlier examples of the genre chiefly in its explicit treatment of the central erotic relationship. The director is a specialist in the *polar* and Robin Cook, writer of the original novel, is another example of an 'Anglo-Saxon' author whose work is popular in the *Série Noire*.

PANIQUE
[PANIC]

1946. bw. 96 mins.
d. Julien Duvivier
sc. Duvivier, Charles Spaak from the novel *Les Fiancailles de M.*

Hire by Simenon
ph. Nicolas Hayer
m. Jacques Ibert
p. Filmsonor
with: Michel Simon, Viviane Romance, Paul Bernard, Charles Dorat

A girl is murdered and suspicion falls on an innocent man (Simon). Patrice Leconte's remake, *Monsieur Hire*, shifted the emphasis away from the plot by the real killer to make the central character of Hire more ambiguous. Duvivier's version is remarkable chiefly for the performance by Simon, one of the great originals of French cinema, who was never guilty of understating a role.

PÉRIL EN LA DEMEURE
[DEATH IN A FRENCH GARDEN]

1985. 101 mins.
d. Michel Deville
sc. Deville, Rosaline Damamme from René Belleto's novel *Sur la terre comme au ciel*
ph. Martial Thury
m. Brahms, Granados, Schubert
p. Gaumont/TF1/Eléfilm
with: Christophe Malavoy, Nicole Garcia, Richard Bohringer, Anémone, Michel Piccoli

A young man (Malavoy) agrees to give music lessons to the daughter of a bourgeois couple (Piccoli, Garcia) and is drawn into a deadly erotic game. An attack on the bourgeoisie, with a plot so intricate as to be largely incomprehensible.

PICKPOCKET

1959. bw. 80 mins.
d. Robert Bresson
sc. Bresson

ph. Léonce-Henri Burel
m. Lulli
ad. P. Charbonnier
p. Lux
with: Martin La Salle, Marika Green, Kassagi, Jean Pelegri

A young man (La Salle) embarks on a career as a pickpocket and, despite the warnings of a police inspector (Pelegri), becomes obsessed and takes lessons from a professional (Kassagi). But, falling in love with a young girl (Green), he flees to London. Bresson, as usual, employs mainly unknown actors to tell an austere tale of redemption, clearly inspired by Dostoyevski's *Crime and Punishment*, in which hands, objects and sounds tell the story. 'The acting that he has managed to coax from a non-professional is miraculous,' Cocteau wrote, adding that the central character has the 'existential terror of an animal stalking its prey and fearful of being stalked in its turn.'

PIERROT LE FOU

1965. 110 mins.
d. Jean-Luc Godard
sc. Godard from Lionel White's novel *Obsession*
ph. Raoul Coutard
m. Antoine Duhamel
p. Beauregard/Laurentiis
with: Jean-Pierre Belmondo, Anna Karina

Pierrot (Belmondo), bored with life in Paris, leaves his wife and child, and spends the night with a young woman (Karina). He wakes up to find a corpse in her flat and they set off towards the South of France, robbing and killing as they go. Larded with references to other movies and to political events, this has been interpreted as a tragedy about the impermanence of love, 'stupendous tedium' (Dilys Powell), 'the best French film of the year' (Georges Sadoul), 'the order of disorder' (Aragon), by a director who is 'consistent in his inconsistency' (Jean-Pierre Jeancolas) and whose characters 'surrender deliberately to a cold lunacy' (Powell) in 'a relationship that is equal parts nonsense and despair' (Chris Auty). 'It seems to me that . . . he has reached a stage at which self-confidence and self-indulgence join hands to lead him into a disaster area.' (Powell, April 1966).

PLEIN SOLEIL
[PURPLE NOON]

1959. 115 mins.
d. René Clément
sc. Clément, Paul Gégauff from Patricia Highsmith's novel *The Talented Mr Ripley*
ph. Henri Decaë
m. Nino Rota
p. Paris/Panitalia/Titanus
with: Alain Delon, Maurice Ronet, Marie Laforest, Elvire Popesco

The friend (Delon) of a playboy (Ronet) plans to kill him and steal the trappings of his luxurious life. Patricia Highsmith's work has been popular with European directors. Her amoral character, Ripley, reappeared in Wim Wenders' *The American Friend* (1977, played by Dennis Hopper) and *This Sweet Sickness* was adapted in 1977 by Claude Miller (under the title *Dîtes-lui que je l'aime*, with Gérard Depardieu in the lead). *Plein soleil* was Delon's first major success and illustrated his potential in the role of a cold, ruthless killer.

PLEINS FEUX SUR L'ASSASSIN

1960. bw. 95 mins.
d. Georges Franju
sc. Pierre Boileau, Thomas Narcejac
ph. Marcel Fradetal
m. Maurice Jarre

ad. Roger Biraucourt
p. Champs-Elysées
with: Pierre Brasseur, Marianne Koch, Dany Saval, Jean-Louis Trintignant, Pascale Audret

Rich relatives hope to inherit the family home and possessions from the Comte de Kéraudon (Brasseur), so he arranges that his body should not be found, preventing the inheritance from being released and obliging them to maintain the estate. They organize '*son et lumière*' spectacles to raise money; then a murder takes place. Franju's film is a mixture of country house detective mystery and gothic horror, though he complained that his producers would not allow him to give free rein to his surrealist fantasy. The scriptwriters, Boileau and Narcejac (quoted in Raymond Durgnat's *Franju*), remarked that the detective story, 'far from being a purely cerebral diversion . . . unleashes the noctural and animal forces of the imagination . . . [and] enables them to feel all the ambiguous aspects of a world which we wrongly believe to be purified of all magic . . .'

POLICE

1985. 109 mins.
d. Maurice Pialat
sc. Pialat, Catherine Breillat, Sylvie Danton, Jacques Fieschi
ph. Luciano Tovoli
m. Henryk Gorecki
ad. Constantin Mejinsky
p. Emmanuel Schlumberger/Gaumont/TF1
with: Gérard Depardieu, Sophie Marceau, Sandrine Bonnaire, Richard Anconina

Inspector Mangin (Depardieu) tries to infiltrate and break a Tunisian drug ring in Belleville, but falls in love with the girlfriend (Marceau) of one of the members. A mixture of semi-documentary and love story, which did not please the police force because of Mangin's brutal methods of interrogation and his open admission that he takes bribes. Depardieu won the award for Best Actor at the Venice Film Festival in his first role on the right side of the law (though he reportedly refused to prepare for it by watching the police at work, because of his dislike of them).

POLICE PYTHON 357

1976. bw. 125 mins.
d. Alain Corneau
sc. Corneau, Daniel Boulanger
ph. Etienne Becker
p. Albina
with: Yves Montand, François Perier, Simone Signoret, Stefania Sandrinelli, Mathieu Carrière

Inspector Ferrot (Montand) investigates the murder of a young woman with whom he was in love, but who was also the mistress of his superior; the trail constantly leads back to Ferrot himself. Set in Orléans, this is a story of self-discovery and alienation by a modern director who has made an important contribution to the genre and made use of some excellent writers: Boulanger for this film and for *La Menace* (1977); Georges Perec for *Série noire* (1979; q.v.).

POULET AU VINAIGRE
[COP AU VIN]

1984. 109 mins.
d. Claude Chabrol
sc. Chabrol, Dominique Roulet
ph. Jean Rabier
m. Matthieu Chabrol
p. MK2
with: Jean Poiret, Stéphane Audran, Michel Bouquet, Lucas Belvaux

A young postman (Belvaux), who lives in a small provincial

town with his crippled mother (Audran) turns sleuth to find the murderer of a businessman who has been threatening to buy up their house. Then Inspector Lavardin (Poiret) arrives. A clever English title (*poulet*, 'chicken', is a slang word for policeman) and an ending in which justice is done, despite the letter of the law. Otherwise, a typical Chabrolian analysis of the small-town bourgeoisie. Chabrol liked the character enough to make a sequel with Poiret, *Inspecteur Lavardin* (q.v.).

QUAI DES ORFÈVRES
[JENNY LAMOUR]

1947. bw. 105mins.
d. Henri-Georges Clouzot
sc. Clouzot, Jean Ferry from the novel by S. A. Steeman
ph. Armand Thirard
m. Francis Lopez
ad. Max Douy
p. Majestic
with: Louis Jouvet, Suzy Delair, Bernard Blier, Simone Renant, Charles Dullin

A police inspector (Jouvet) tackles his last case before retirement. The lover (Dullin) of a music-hall singer (Delair) is found dead by her husband (Blier), who is persuaded that she is the killer. Clouzot delights in the sordid settings (café-concert, police stations and apartments), and gave Jouvet, the leading French actor of his generation, a splendid final cinema role as the world-weary, but sympathetic inspector. 'A banal thriller plot,' Georges Sadoul said, but filmed with a sense of atmosphere and suspense worthy of Hitchcock; Thirard's photography at times recalled Manet, Degas and Toulouse-Lautrec, overshadowing 'some dark reflections on morals and behaviour'. The explicit treatment of sex (one character is lesbian) is one thing that distinguished French cinema from British or American films of the period.

QUE LA BÊTE MEURE
[THIS MAN MUST DIE/KILLER!]

1969. 110 mins.
d. Claude Chabrol
sc. Paul Gégauff from the novel *The Beast Must Die* by Nicholas Blake (C. Day Lewis)
ph. Jean Rabier
m. Pierre Jansen
ad. Guy Littaye
p. Les Films La Boétie/Rizzoli
with: Michel Duchaussoy, Caroline Cellier, Jean Yanne, Anouk Ferjac, Marc Di Napoli, Maurice Pialat

A widower, Charles (Duchaussoy), hunts the hit-and-run driver who has killed his only son, and becomes involved with a woman (Cellier) whose brother-in-law, Paul (Yanne), is his chief suspect. Then the brutish Paul is murdered by his own son (Di Napoli) and Charles takes the blame. A complex web of guilt, revenge and transfer of feelings — Chabrol's 'most Langian film', according to Phil Hardy in the *Time Out Film Guide*, with a final scene which Michael Walker judged to be 'an almost literal recreation of the ending of *Moonfleet*'.

RENÉ-LA-CANNE

1977. 100 mins.
d. Francis Girod
sc. Girod, Jacques Rouffio from the book by Roger Borniche
ph. Aldo Tonti
m. Ennio Morricone
p. G. Crosnier/Luciano Piperino
with: Gérard Depardieu, Michel Piccoli, Sylvia Kristel

René (Depardieu), a small-time crook, is arrested during the Occupation and sent to a psychiatric hospital where he meets a policeman (Piccoli) hiding from the Germans. After various adventures in a work camp, also involving Kristel, they separate, but meet up again after the Liberation. A confused attempt to make a satire on the police that is also a sex comedy and a vehicle for its three stars.

LES RIPOUX
[LE COP]

1985. 106 mins
d. Claude Zidi
sc. Zidi, Didier Kaminka
ph. Jean-Jacques Tarbes
m. Francis Lai
p. Film 7
with: Philippe Noiret, Thierry Lhermitte, Régine

Inspector René (Noiret), whose main interests are gambling on the horses and enjoying a quiet life, contributes to the sum of human happiness in his quarter of Paris by turning a blind eye to small-time criminal activities in exchange for a reasonable cut on the proceeds; but all this is threatened when he gets a new partner (Lhermitte), an ambitious young graduate of the police academy. Eventually the two develop an understanding and a father-son relationship. The amoral René, a relative of the policeman played by Piccoli in *René-la-Canne*, represents the French ideal of the mildly corruptible man on the beat and the comedy was a popular success. The alternative, in this and its sequel, is shown to be a far more vicious and rapacious breed of *flic*, the message being that it is better to live and let live.

LE SALAIRE DE LA PEUR
[THE WAGES OF FEAR]

1953. bw. 140 mins.
d. Henri-Georges Clouzot
sc. Clouzot from the novel by Georges Arnaud
ph. Armand Thirard
m. Georges Auric
ad. René Renoux
p. Filmsonor/CICC/Vera
with: Yves Montand, Charles Vanel, Folco Lulli, Peter van Eyck

Four exiles (Montand, Vanel, Lulli, van Eyck), longing to escape from a grim South American township, are hired to drive two lorries loaded with nitroglycerine to an oilfield where the explosive is needed to put out a fire; but the mountain roads are largely unmade and the slightest jolt threatens to blow up the nitroglycerine. 'An epic, with the stress on courage and its antithesis' (Clouzot). One of the most successful French films ever, it won awards for Best Film at Cannes and Berlin. The final shock in the ending attracted criticism, though it was defended by Bernard Dort, in *Les Temps modernes*, June 1953: 'debatable in terms of simple credibility, but an astounding metaphor, carrying us from the realm of necessity to that of myth'. Most of all, however, Clouzot was attacked for his grim portrayal of the human condition. The Centrale Catholique du Cinéma rated it: 'For adults, with reservations' and Gilbert Salachas (*Télé-Ciné*, 40-41, 1954) called it deliberately negative, morally unhealthy, aggressively despairing and nihilistic, quoting Pierre Kast's (presumably approving) view that it was 'a great atheist film'. We admired Clouzot for cleaning away 'the Marseille fog of the French films of the Thirties,' Pauline Kael wrote, comparing Clouzot's existentialism favourably with that of Alain Renais in *La Guerre est finie*; but there was strong reaction in the United States to the implied anti-imperialism in the film's depiction of an American oil company in an (unnamed) banana republic.

LE SAMOURAÏ

1967. 95 mins.
d. Jean-Pierre Melville
sc. Melville, Georges Pellegrin
ph. Henri Decaë
m. François de Robaix
p. Filmel/CICC/Fida
with: Alain Delon, Cathy Rosier, François Périer, Nathalie Delon

A contract killer (Delon) is pursued by police and gangsters after a murder, and ordered to kill the witness (Rosier) who might identify him, even though she has refused to do so. A superb performance by Delon as the icy professional, in a film that influenced a number of Hollywood movies (Martin Scorsese's *Taxi Driver*, 1976), as well as drawing on earlier American *film noir*. An austere study of an outsider, taking to the extreme the notion of the criminal's code of behaviour and honour as a morality which is internally consistent, however much it conflicts with accepted social norms.

LE SCANDALE
[THE CHAMPAGNE MURDERS]

1967. 110 mins.
d. Claude Chabrol
sc. Claude Brulé, Derek Prouse, Paul Gégauff
ph. Jean Rabier
m. Pierre Jansen
p. Universal
with: Anthony Perkins, Maurice Ronet, Stéphane Audran, Yvonne Furneaux, Suzanne Lloyd

A playboy (Ronet) is tricked into believing that he is a

murderer by the owner of a champagne company (Furneaux), her husband (Perkins) and her secretary (Audran). A film of Chabrol's 'commercial period', made in French and English versions, with a depressing view of human nature and a ludicrously convoluted plot (Anthony Perkins said he agreed to play in it only in order to work out who was the killer; it is not certain whether he succeeded). 'The film's "normal" characters (in so far as the word is applicable at all) are entirely repellent,' according to Robin Wood.

LE SECRET

1974. 102 mins.
d. Robert Enrico
sc. Pascal Jardin
ph. Etienne Becker
m. Ennio Morricone
p. President/Euro International
with: Jean-Louis Trintignant, Marlène Jobert, Philippe Noiret

A fugitive (Trintignant) takes refuge at the isolated home of a couple (Jobert, Noiret) and tells them that he is the victim of a government conspiracy: is he genuine, or mad? A suspenseful thriller by the director of the short, *La Rivière d'Hibou [Incident at Owl Creek*, 1961].

SÉRIE NOIRE

1979. 110 mins.
d. Alain Corneau
sc. Georges Perec from Jim Thompson's novel *A Hell of a Woman*
ph. Pierre-William Glenn
p. Prospectacle/Gaumont
with: Patrick Dewaere. Myriam Boyer, Marie Trintignant, Bernard Blier

Frank, a door-to-door salesman (Dewaere), murders the

aunt of his girl-friend (Trintignant) to steal the money that he needs to pay his debts, but becomes the victim of a blackmailer (Blier). Transferring the action of Thompson's thriller from the American South to the bleak landscape of the Parisian suburbs, Corneau's film is not so much a tribute to Hollywood *film noir* as to its influence on the alienated central character, brilliantly scripted by Georges Perec in an elaborate slang which is itself a comment on Frank's search for identity through language.

LA SIRÈNE DU MISSISSIPPI
[THE MISSISSIPPI MERMAID]

1969. 123 mins.
d. François Truffaut
sc. Truffaut from the novel *Waltz Into Darkness* by William Irish (Cornell Woolrich)
ph. Denys Clerval
m. Antoine Duhamel
p. Les Films du Carrosse/Artistes Associés/Delphos
with: Jean-Paul Belmondo, Catherine Deneuve, Michel Bouquet

A factory owner (Belmondo) on the island of Réunion advertises for a wife, and gets an imposter and *femme fatale* (Deneuve). As Truffaut pointed out in a letter to the distributor Roger Diamantis (April 5, 1971), the film reverses the usual expectations about the couple's physical relationship, by making the man the innocent and the woman the experienced partner. It is stacked with references to other films, including Belmondo's characters in *A bout de souffle* and *Pierrot le fou*, as well as to Truffaut's own earlier explorations of love and obsession.

1985. 102 mins.
d. Luc Besson
sc. Besson, Pierre Jolivet, Alain Le Henry, Sophie Schmit, Marc Perrier
ph. Carlo Carini
m. Eric Serra
ad. Alexandre Trauner
p. Films du Loup/TSF/TF1
with: Christophe Lambert, Isabelle Adjani, Richard Bohringer, Michel Galabru, Jean-Hugues Anglade

A thief (Lambert) steals important documents and goes into hiding among the drop-outs who live in the passageways behind the métro, inducing the wife (Adjani) of one of the crooks to follow him. A highly successful, glossy thriller by a 26-year old director, which makes good use of its subterranean setting, and picks up a familiar theme of Parisian thrillers: the parallel world that is supposed to exist just behind the surface of everyday life.

TENDRE POULET
[DEAR DETECTIVE]

1977. 105 mins.
d. Philippe de Broca
sc. de Broca, Michel Audiard
ph. Jean-Paul Schwartz
m. Georges Delerue
p. Ariane/Mondex
with: Annie Girardot, Philippe Noiret

A police inspector (Girardot) knocks over a classics teacher (Noiret) and falls in love with him, while investigating a murder. A charming and light-hearted comedy, plus thriller, notable for having a woman in the detective role (as the title suggests).

THÉRÈSE DESQUEYROUX

1962. bw. 109 mins.
d. Georges Franju
sc. Franju, François Mauriac, Claude Mauriac from F. Mauriac's novel
ph. Christian Matras
m. Maurice Jarre
p. Filmel
with: Emmanuele Riva, Philippe Noiret, Edith Scob, Sami Frey

Stifled by the tedium of provincial life, Thérèse (Riva) tries to poison her husband (Noiret). Taken from a novel by a noted modern catholic writer and made by a noted atheist director, the film met with a mixed critical reception. Jean Douchet (*Cahiers du cinéma*, Oct. 1962) felt it was a mistake to update the story from the 1920s, and described it as 'anti-bourgeois, anti-religion and anti-society'. *Positif* called it 'stiff' and 'bloodless'. The meeting between Franju and Mauriac has been interpreted as a case of the writer not knowing what the director was doing to his work, but in reality illustrates an element of pessimism and existentialism in French catholic thinking. Catholics like Mauriac and Bresson are preoccupied with evil and original sin, to the point where their outlook on the universe may at times seem indistinguishable from disbelief. Jansenism and Calvinism are not a bad basis for *film noir*.

THÉRÈSE RAQUIN
[THE ADULTERESS]

1953. bw. 110 mins.
d. Marcel Carné
sc. Carné, Charles Spaak
ph. Roger Hubert
m. Maurice Thiriet
ad. Paul Bertrand
p. Paris/Lux

with: Simone Signoret, Jacques Duby, Raf Vallone, Roland Lesaffre, Anna-Maria Casilio

The wife (Signoret) of a railway worker (Duby) falls for a truck driver (Vallone) and the lovers arrange for the husband to fall off a train, but a veteran of the war in Indochina (Lesaffre) has enough evidence to blackmail them; and it is to be his accidental death that finally destroys them. Carné updated Emile Zola's original (already filmed in 1915 by Nino Martoglio and in 1928 by Jacques Feyder), and moved it to Lyon, for what is generally considered his best post-war film, a nineteenthth-century novel reinterpreted through the lens of such *films noirs* as *The Postman Always Rings Twice*.

TIREZ SUR LE PIANISTE
[SHOOT THE PIANO PLAYER]

1960. bw. 80mins.
d. François Truffaut
sc. Truffaut, Marcel Moussy from the novel *Down There* by David Goodis
ph. Raoul Coutard
m. Georges Delerue
p. Les Films de la Pléiade
with: Charles Aznavour, Marie Dubois, Nicole Berger, Michèle Mercier

A nightclub pianist (Aznavour) helps his brothers to escape from gangsters, but involves his girlfriend (Dubois) in an intrigue that will eventually lead to her death. A homage to the Hollywood B-movie, made in the style of the early New Wave, much like Godard.

TOUCHEZ PAS AU GRISBI
[GRISBI/HONOUR AMONG THIEVES]

1954. bw. 90 mins.
d. Jacques Becker
sc. Becker, Maurice Griffe, Albert Simonin from Simonin's novel
ph. Pierre Montazel
m. Jean Wiener
ad. Jean d'Eaubonne
p. Del Duca/Silver/Antarès
with: Jean Gabin, René Dary, Paul Frankeur, Lino Ventura, Jeanne Moreau, Dora Doll, Victor Franken

A thief (Gabin), planning to retire on the proceeds of an airport gold robbery, is forced to hand over the loot as ransom for a friend (Dary) who has been kidnapped by a rival gang. One of the most influential and effective post-war gangster films, the lead superbly played by Gabin (who won the award for Best Actor at the Venice Festival), exploring the morality of the underworld, its rivalries as a form of war and its money ethos as a form of business.

TRANS-EUROP-EXPRESS

1966. bw. 90 mins.
d. Alain Robbe-Grillet
sc. Robbe-Grillet
ph. Willy Kurant
m. Verdi
p. Como
with: Jean-Lous Trintignant, Marie-France Pisier, Robbe-Grillet, Nadine Verdier, Christian Barbier, Catherine Robbe-Grillet

A writer (Robbe-Grillet) on the train from Paris to Antwerp is writing a screenplay about a smuggler (Trintignant) going to collect a consignment of drugs and becoming involved in a sadistic relationship with a prostitute (Pisier). A leading exponent of the *Nouveau roman* decides to explore some of his fantasies in what is ostensibly a thriller set aboard the Paris-Antwerp express, in the certainty that it will generate a lot of pretentious criticism. It does.

LE TROU
[THE HOLE]

1959. bw. 83 mins.
d. Jacques Becker
sc. Becker, Jean Aurel, José Giovanni from Giovanni's novel
ph. Ghislain Cloquet
p. Play-Art/Filmsonor/Titanus
with: Michel Constantin, Philippe Leroy, Marc Michel, Jean Keraudy, Raymond Meunier

Four prisoners on remand in La Santé are plotting to escape, but their plans are threatened by the arrival of a newcomer (Michel). Made with no background music, using amateur actors and based on a true story, Becker's last work is a Bressonian tale of craftsmanship and betrayal, which Georges Sadoul described as 'a noble and virile work'. Most critics agreed, speaking of 'austerity' and 'rigour', and making the inevitable comparisons with *Un Condamné à mort s'est échappé*. However, it was not a box office success.

UN CONDAMNÉ A MORT S'EST ÉCHAPPÉ
[A MAN ESCAPED]

1956. bw. 102 mins.
d. Robert Bresson
sc. Bresson based on the story of André Devigny
ph. Léonce-Henri Burel
m. Mozart
p. GAU/SNE
with: François Leterrier, Charles Le Clainche

A member of the Resistance (Leterrier), condemned to death

and imprisoned at the fortress of Montluc, plans to escape with his young cellmate (Le Clainche). André Bazin called it 'a work unlike any other'; François Truffaut: 'the most crucial French film in the past ten years'. The film that established Bresson's reputation in Europe and won him the award for Best Director at Cannes, it was a failure in the United States. Pauline Kael ('a marvellous movie') suggested that this was probably because American audiences expected escape films to be about action.

UN CONDÉ
[THE COP]

1970. 98 mins.
d. Yves Boisset
sc. Boisset, Claude Veillot
ph. Jean-Marc Ripert
m. Antoine Duhamel
p. Stephen Films/Empire Films
with: Michel Bouquet, Françoise Fabian, Gianni Garko, Michel Constantin

The murder of a nightclub owner and an attack on his sister (Fabian) is revenged by her lover (Garko), leading to a gang war involving the police. The violence and depiction of a police force in collusion with organized crime were controversial.

UNE SI JOLIE PETITE PLAGE
[RIPTIDE]

1949. bw. 91 mins.
d. Yves Allégret
sc. Jacques Sigurd
ph. Henri Alekan
m. Maurice Thiriet, Sigurd
p. CICC/Dormer/Corona

with: Gérard Philipe, Madeleine Robinson, Jane Marken, Jean Servais

An orphan (Philipe) returns to the Norman seaside hotel where he worked some years before and was mistreated by the owner (Marken). He falls in love with a chambermaid (Robinson), but one of the other guests (Servais) knows that he has committed a murder. Rainswept, doom-laden post-war thriller, 'Allégret's best *film noir*' (Sadoul), inevitably recalling the Carné-Prévert films of the 1930s.

LES VALSEUSES
[MAKING IT/GOING PLACES]

1974. 118 mins.
d. Bertrand Blier
sc. Blier, Philippe Dumarçay
ph. Bruno Nuytten
m. Stéphane Grappelli
p. CAPAC/UPF/SN
with: Gérard Depardieu, Patrick Dewaere, Miou-Miou, Jeanne Moreau

Two young tearaways (Depardieu, Dewaere) go joy-riding in a stolen car. When they decide to return it, they find themselves confronted by the owner with a gun, so they tie him up and abduct his girlfriend (Miou-Miou). A caper movie, with lots of bad language, sex and violence, it did a good deal to establish the screen personae of Depardieu and Dewaere, and was highly popular with French audiences. In Britain, it was banned from general release and only given a limited showing in London, but was revived in 1992.

THE VANISHING

1988. 104 mins.
d. George Sluizer
sc. Sluizer, Tim Krabbé from Krabbé's novel *The Golden Egg*
ph. Toni Kuhn
m. Henri Vrienten
p. Golden Egg/Ingrid/MGS
with: Gene Bervoets, Bernard-Pierre Donnadieu, Johanna Ter Steege

A Dutch couple are driving to the holiday home they have rented in France when they stop at a service station. The woman (Ter Steege) goes to buy some soft drinks and does not return. The man, Rex (Bervoets), searches for her in desperation and, three years later, is still obsessed with finding out what has happened. Then his appeals for help are answered by the murderer (Donnadieu), who promises to end Rex's uncertainty. A Dutch-French co-production, its inclusion here is justified by a clear debt to the French tradition of the psychological thriller. The audience is never in doubt about the perpetrator of the crime; the focus is on the personality of the killer behind his mundane façade, the game that he plays with Rex and the implied identification between them: both are driven by intellectual needs that override their emotional ones (and, in Rex's case, the instinct for self-preservation). Because of the film's success, Sluizer was invited to remake it in Hollywood in 1993, with an American setting and some changes to the plot to ensure its acceptability to the American market.

LA VEUVE COUDERC

1971.
d. Pierre Granier-Deferre
sc. Granier-Deferre, Pascal Jardin from the novel by Simenon
ph. Walter Wottitz
m. Philippe Sarde

p. Lira
with: Simone Signoret, Alain Delon, Jean Tissier

A widow (Signoret), living alone on her farm in Burgundy during the 1920s, shelters a man (Delon) hunted by the police. A fairly banal story improved by good colour photography and an interesting rural setting.

LA VIE, L'AMOUR, LA MORT
[LIFE, LOVE, DEATH]

1969. 115 mins.
d. Claude Lelouch
sc. Lelouch, Pierre Uytterhoeven
ph. Jean Collomb
m. Francis Lai
p. Les Films 13/Ariane/Artistes Associés/PEA
with: Amidou, Janine Magnan, Caroline Cellier, Marcel Bozzuffi

A North African factory worker (Amidou) is condemned to death for the murder of a prostitute who has taunted him with his sexual inadequacies. Mixing black-and-white and colour, Lelouch compiles a grim indictment of the death penalty, 17 years after André Cayatte's *Nous sommes tous des assassins* (q.v.), with the emphasis again on the obscenity of the ritual leading the condemned man to his final moments. Capital punishment was not finally ended in France until 1981 (though it had been only rarely applied for some time before that), so Lelouch's film was a contribution to the debate on abolition. Marcel Martin in *Les Lettres françaises*, January 1971, raised a frequent objection to the film: that the sympathetic treatment of the central character was a form of special pleading, obviously weighting the case in his favour. Lelouch's earlier films had given him a reputation for romanticism, though critics noted that here he uses a more controlled camera style and introduces a note of genuine compassion, as opposed to sentimentality.

VIVEMENT DIMANCHE
[CONFIDENTIALLY YOURS]

1983. bw. 117 mins.
d. François Truffaut
sc. Truffaut, Suzanne Schiffman, Jean Aurel from the novel *The Long Saturday Night* by Charles Williams
ph. Nestor Almendros
m. Georges Delerue
p. Les Films du Carrosse/A2/Sorpofilms
with: Fanny Ardent, Jean-Louis Trintignant, Jean-Pierre Kalfon, Philippe Laudenbach

An estate agent (Trintignant) is accused of murdering his wife and goes into hiding while his secretary (Ardent) sets out to prove his innocence. A comedy-thriller on a well-worn theme, the director's last film was an obvious homage to the Hollywood thrillers of the 1940s (the source is a typical *Série Noire* novel and the photography is in black-and-white). 'Every story is a tall story,' Truffaut said.

LE VOLEUR
[THE THIEF OF PARIS]

1967. 120 mins.
d. Louis Malle
sc. Malle, Jean-Claude Carrière, Daniel Boulanger from the novel by Georges Darien
ph. Henri Decaë
p. Nouvelles Editions de Films/Artistes Associés/Montoro
with: Jean-Paul Belmondo, Geneviève Bujold, Marie Dubois, Julien Guiomar, Christian Lude

Georges Randal (Belmondo) is an orphan in Paris at the turn of the century who has been tricked out of his inheritance by his uncle (Lude) and foiled in his plan to marry his cousin (Bujold). He turns to a life of crime, with the help of an underworld boss, the Abbé La Margelle (Guiomar). Casting Belmondo against type (at the time) as the dandyish central character, Malle suggests the political and social implications of this 'gentleman thief' story, from a little-known novel which contains elements of Surrealism, anarchism and anti-clericalism. The film was not liked by the critics — Malle suggested that this was because the mood in the late 1960s was hostile to what appeared to be simply an amusing period drama.

WEEKEND

1967. 105 mins.
d. Jean-Luc Godard
sc. Godard
ph. Raoul Coutard
m. Mozart, Antoine Duhamel
p. Lira/Comacico/Copernic/Ascot Cineraid
with: Mireille Darc, Jean Yanne, Jean-Pierre Léaud, Juliet Berto, Anne Wiazemsky

A couple (Yanne, Darc), incidentally plotting a middle-class murder to gain an inheritance, set off from Paris by car and are caught up in a nightmare landscape littered with corpses and burning vehicles, before emerging into the woods where a group of guerrilla fighters are plotting to overthrow the bourgeois state and the consumer society that it has spawned, while reverting to cannibalism. Godard's pre-1968 fable was Swiftian and savagely prophetic, with some flashes of genuine black humour. 'Horror at violence can be carried out without resort to actual violence,' Dilys Powell wrote, with particular reference to the scene of cutting a pig's throat. ' . . . I distrust the pacifism of people who make their protests by violence.' Unlike Godard's films of the 1970s, however, it did have a comprehensible storyline and kept its political sermons for the last half-hour or so.

LES YEUX SANS VISAGE
[THE HORROR CHAMBER OF DR FAUSTUS]

1959. bw. 90 mins.
d. Georges Franju
sc. Franju, Jean Redon, Claude Sautet, Pierre Boileau, Thomas Narcejac from Redon's novel
ph. Eugen Shufftan
m. Maurice Jarre
ad. Auguste Capelier
p. Champs-Elysées/Lux
with: Pierre Brasseur, Alida Valli, Edith Scob, François Guérin

After his daughter (Scob) is disfigured in a car crash, a plastic surgeon (Brasseur) and his assistant (Valli) murder young women to provide the skin tissue for him to graft a new face. A horror film, heavily influenced by German Expressionism — and perhaps by Cocteau, who praised Franju for not forgetting 'the golden rule, which is to apply the greatest possible realism to the depiction of the unreal. The awful thing about *Les Yeux sans visage* is that we believe in it.' An attack on the bourgeois (and, Raymond Durgnat suggests, Pétainist) idea of the family? A gothic horror? A critique of the misuse of science to be compared with Mary Shelley? Franju illustrates the long ancestry of the horror film, as well as its links with the thriller and *film noir*, and the ability of all these genres to examine important questions and to touch nerves. The British press hated the film: Durgnat wrote that 'in England, *Les Yeux sans visage* was greeted with a unanimously shocked, or contemptuous press . . . Almost the only reviewer in a national daily to give it a good review very nearly lost her job as a result . . . Needless to say, *Sight and Sound* bayed its utter scorn . . . ' The title *The Horror Chamber of Dr Faustus* was the one given to an American dubbed version.

1968. 125 mins.
d. Costa-Gavras
sc. Costa-Gavras, Jorge Semprun from the novel by Vassili Vassilikos
ph. Raoul Coutard
m. Mikis Theodorakis
p. Reggane/ONCIC
with: Yves Montand, Irene Papas, Jean-Louis Trintignant, Jacques Perrin, François Périer

The leader of an opposition party (Montand) is knocked down by a car after a political rally and dies. The investigating magistrate (Trintignant) undercovers a wide-ranging government plot. Based on the case of Gregory Lambrakis, the Greek opposition deputy who was killed in May 1963, Costa-Gavras' film won the Oscar for Best Foreign Film and was seen as virtually establishing a new genre of political thriller. Pauline Kael, in the *New Yorker*, pointed out the parallels with such films as *Cornered, Brute Force* and *Crossfire*. Some critics were unhappy with the mixture of thriller and political message, either because they found the film propagandist, or else because they felt it sacrificed too much to the genre. In general, however, the criticism was favourable: Henry Chapier in *Combat* said that there had not been a political film as fine and pure as *Z* in the previous twenty years. It was not shown in Greece until 1974.

BIBLIOGRAPHY

Cameron, Iaqn (ed.) *The Movie Book of Film Noir*, Studio Vista, London, 1992.

Durgnat, Raymond, *Franju*, University of California Press, California, 1967.

Forbes, Jill, *The Cinema in France after the New Wave*, Macmillan/BFI, London, 1992.

Kael, Pauline, *Kiss Kiss Bang Bang*, Marion Boyars, London, 1970; *Taking It All In*, Marion Boyars, London, 1986.

Malle, Louis & French, Philip, *Malle on Malle*, Faber, London, 1993.

Nogueira, Rui, *Le Cinéma français*, Flammarion, Paris, 1962.

Sadoul, Georges, *Dictionnaire des films*, du Seuil, Paris, 1965 (revised 1990).

Various, *The Time Out Film Guide*, Penguin, London, 1991.

Wood, Robin & Walker, Martin, *Chabrol*, Studio Vista, London, 1970.

INDEX